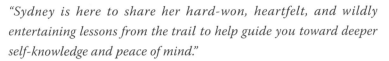

"Sydney is here to share her hard-won, heartfelt, and wildly entertaining lessons from the trail to help guide you toward deeper self-knowledge and peace of mind."

–Gale Straub, author of *She Explores: Stories of Life-Changing Adventures on the Road and in the Wild*

"Like any good hike, this book is an adventure. Sydney beautifully takes us on a journey with her as she hikes her feelings and discovers what it means to be whole again."

–Anastasia Allison, founder of Kula Cloth®

"Williams' candid storytelling and personal anecdotes make you feel like you're hiking alongside her, sharing in her moments of vulnerability and growth. Hiking Your Feelings *is a compelling call to embrace both our inner landscapes and the world that surrounds us."*

–Kenya Jackson-Saulters, M.S., Chief Experience Officer of the Outdoor Journal Tour and author of *Nature Meditations Deck: Simple Mindfulness Practices Inspired by the Natural World*

"Through sharing her journey, Sydney is able to help others navigate their own challenges. In this book, we see firsthand the transformation that nature can provide."

–Sirena Rana, author of *Best Day Hikes on the Arizona National Scenic Trail* and founder of Trails Inspire

"Hiking Your Feelings helps the traveler turn reflective miles into heartfelt smiles. Hiking includes both ups and downs, but when it's done as described in this book, you can be confident in both your journey and your destination."

–Wayne S. Dysinger, M.D., M.P.H., former president of the American College of Lifestyle Medicine

To the Trailblazers, Cycle-Breakers,
Truth-Tellers, and Survivors:

Thank you for lighting the way. Your very presence
has forever changed the course of human progress,
and for that, I am eternally grateful.

HIKING
YOUR
FEELINGS

BLAZING A TRAIL TO SELF-LOVE

SYDNEY WILLIAMS

FOREWORD BY GLADYS MCGAREY, M.D.

MANDALA

SAN RAFAEL LOS ANGELES LONDON

CONTENTS

FOREWORD

Hiking Your Feelings: Blazing a Trail to Self-Love is one of the most helpful self-journeys I have run across in my 102 years. Sydney Williams has created within these pages a menu to satisfy the appetite of every hungry reader. Trauma is common to the human experience. And Sydney has tasted more than her share. Here, she not only shares her personal experiences with open and sometimes brutal honesty, but she also offers a framework within which she was able not to *get over* her trauma, but rather to *live through* it. She calls this framework "hiking her feelings."

Her willingness to go deep and share openly about the painful trauma of her life is a part of what makes this book such a rare find. Quite often, a book will appear that deals with a person's challenges with a particular trauma. Many books are available that address, from one perspective or another, such traumas as struggles with weight loss, struggles with self-esteem and body image, the adjustment in lifestyle that comes when a person is diagnosed with diabetes, or the struggles related to being or not being successful in one sport or another. Books are now starting to rise to the surface about the personal journeys of those who have experienced sexual assault and are willing to talk about it. Sydney has experienced all of these traumas and more. And she is ready and willing to talk about them. Not just talk about them, but let the reader journey with her and see how she came out on the other side of each one.

Because Sydney has such a rich collection of pain that she has gathered in her life, and because she is so willing to share it with the world through this book, you may find that you have a pain or a trauma in common with Sydney. You will not only connect with her at the level of shared pain, but you will also find herein a proven path for moving through that pain.

Sydney invites you to join her on this journey.

–Dr. Gladys McGarey, M.D.

THE TRAILHEAD

"Sydney?" my husband Barry said, making his way down the narrow hallway from our bedroom toward the kitchen.

Our puggle, Jezebel, was following closely behind, her nails tapping on the linoleum. I made a mental note to trim them on our next day off.

I was mindlessly scanning the contents of the refrigerator, trying to find something to eat before we went to work. "Yeah?"

"I have some bad news." He paused.

I held my breath, feeling time slow down and my chest start to tighten as I waited for him to finish. The pause felt like an entire lifetime, adrenaline coursing through my veins.

"Chris killed himself."

Time stood still. Everything moved in slow motion. I'd been holding my breath, but now I felt like I couldn't breathe at all. I stood up straight and closed the refrigerator door, feeling the cold air whoosh out on my shins as it squished shut. I reluctantly turned toward Barry.

"Are you serious?" I asked, hoping it wasn't true and that I'd misheard him.

He nodded.

I let out a violent exhale as I crumpled to the floor. The light-blue linoleum was cold on my bare legs, sending a chill through my entire body and taking my breath away once more.

I looked up at Barry, my eyes wide with disbelief. I couldn't find words.

While I was in a pile on the floor, Jezebel started licking my face and hopping all over me. Barry knew I wasn't getting up any time soon, so he sat on the floor and held me. The second his arms were around me, all of my defenses came down and I started wailing, sobbing, gasping for breath. Soon enough, both of us were crying. Jezebel stayed close. Chris was one of her favorite humans too.

▪   ▪   ▪   ▪   ▪

I was still grieving Chris—and many other losses—a couple of years later as I sat bobbing on a boat staring at Santa Catalina Island off the coast of Los Angeles, California. Barry and I were going to start hiking the Trans-Catalina Trail (TCT), a thirty-eight-and-a-half-mile backpacking route that spans the island. This was my first backpacking trip, and as I looked at the island looming in the distance, I wondered if I would be able to make it across in one piece. We'd allowed a week for the hike, and I'd bought all the gear I needed, but we hadn't been training at all. For years I'd been a competitive skydiver and in great shape, but those days were over. Working at a standing desk had been the extent of my physical activity lately. When Barry had suggested this trip, I'd questioned my abilities, but he swooped in with logic and reasoning. He told me this would be hard, and reminded me that despite the difficulty, we would just be walking, something I had been doing with some degree of success since I was a toddler. Looking back, the two years leading up to that trip were devastating, but at the time, I had no grasp on the depths of my despair. I was highly functional and able to work, yet at the same time, I was firmly planted in my unhealthy coping mechanisms. I had exactly zero awareness about how proficient I was at doing anything but feeling my feelings.

In this book, I'm going to share how I went from engaging in negative self-talk about myself and my body to loving all of me. About how I shifted my coping mechanisms from eating and drinking my feelings to hiking my feelings. And how you can learn to hike your feelings, too.

Although Catalina is famous for its beautiful ocean views and rugged backcountry, the gift of that first hike (and the second one, a year and a half later) was not just my appreciation of the outer wilderness I climbed, stumbled, and trudged through, but the exploration of my own inner wilderness. These were life-changing experiences that helped me heal my mind and body from trauma and disease. You have a wilderness in you too, and in this book I'm going to offer a framework to help you blaze your own trail to self-love and healing.

GET OUTSIDE

Throughout this book, I'm going to be encouraging you to go for a hike, and I want to be clear here: Please don't think you have to take off on a grand hiking adventure like I did. If you don't have access to hiking trails or if you're just starting out and aren't ready for a big hike yet, it can be as simple as walking around your neighborhood and building from there. Maybe you have a different activity of choice like rock climbing, running, kayaking, fishing, gardening, riding your bike, or paddleboarding. Perhaps you're where I was back in 2016, ass firmly planted on the couch but knowing you're ready to take the next step.

The main thing is to move your body, somewhere outdoors, free from the distractions of this hyperconnected world we're living in. At the very least, leave your headphones at home, save your favorite podcast for another day, and tuck your phone into your pocket or a backpack. By removing the points of connection to technology and the expectations of the society we live in, we can more clearly hear our inner voice and pay attention to the signals our bodies give us.

HIKE YOUR OWN HIKE

"Hike your own hike" serves as a reminder to honor your process. We all start somewhere, and if you're brand new to this, like I was before my first trek on the TCT, I invite you to take an analytical approach to your first few hikes. Pretend you're a scientist and each hike is an experiment. We're just out here collecting data so we can make more informed choices in the future. This is helpful for everything, including trying out new gear, exploring new trails, and hiking with others. If you try on a pair of shoes and they're uncomfortable, exchange them for the proper size. If you're attempting a new (to you) trail and you find yourself running out of energy faster than you thought, make note of the distance that was comfortable for you and dial back the mileage on your next hike. If you're hiking with a group and find yourself pulling up the rear, back of the bus, last in line, resist the temptation to feel like you're less than the faster hikers and revel in what your body is capable of.

On and off the trail, comparison is the thief of joy, and we can have a much more pleasant experience if we allow ourselves to move at our own pace, in our own way.

WELCOME TO YOUR TRAIL OF LIFE

If you haven't discovered this already, one of the things you'll quickly learn is that hiking is a lot like life. There are ups and downs, twists and turns, moments of absolute bliss and beauty, and many moments of struggle. In the Trail of Life section at the end of each chapter, I'll be zooming out from my experiences on the Trans-Catalina Trail and connecting the dots between what was happening on the hike and what had happened in my life. I'll reflect on how the lessons learned along the way helped me blaze my own trail to self-love and how they can help you too.

They say hindsight is twenty-twenty, and we can only connect the dots backward, so we use the Trail of Life to understand where we came from, how we got to where we are today, and how we want to integrate our experiences in the future. In my time facilitating healing journeys in nature for folks from all walks of life, one thing has become clear: When you know where you've been, it's much easier to move forward with an open heart.

UNPACK YOUR TRAUMA PACK

We each carry an invisible backpack full of our experiences on this Trail of Life. I lovingly call this my trauma pack, and for the first three decades of my life, I had no idea I was carrying all of this extra weight. In fact, it wasn't until I started backpacking in 2016 that I was able to slow down enough to tune in to my inner wilderness. As a result, I was able to feel the weight of everything I'd been avoiding. It was heavy.

We're all walking around with our own traumas—and they can be triggered by many different things. In these pages, I'll be sharing about the experiences that filled my trauma pack, the activities and rituals that helped me unpack its contents, and the tools I used to lighten my load. Some of the items in my trauma pack are toxic relationships, body image issues, verbal and emotional abuse, suicide, cancer, sudden death, chronic illness, and sexual assault, to name a few. I also talk about how I almost pooped my pants on the trail, so it's not all doom and gloom. I promise this story ends on a high note.

The items in our trauma packs may be different, but if you're reading this book, the weight of what you've been carrying hasn't crushed you yet. No matter how heavy the load has been, I invite you to take off your trauma pack while you read this book. Feel the burden lift from your shoulders. Roll out your neck. Unclench your jaw. Take a few deep breaths. Settle into a space that feels cozy and safe. You've made it this far. You can do this too.

WHAT YOU'LL NEED

Before any adventure, it's good to do a gear check. There are countless websites, books, courses, and other resources that can point you in the right direction. In the world of hiking and backpacking, they're all going to say approximately the same thing. You'll need a backpack to carry everything for your journey, shelter, water (and/or a way to treat fresh water), food (and a way to prepare it), a sleep system, and the right clothing and footwear.

Noticeably missing from these packing lists and gear reviews are the skills you already possess that are critical for your enjoyment and success. You won't find these items in the store but rather in your mind, body, and spirit:

> **Curiosity:** When embarking on any new endeavor, self-judgment can run rampant if it remains unchecked. The antidote to judgment is curiosity. When things get hard and your inner critic starts barking orders and insults, take a few deep breaths and ask, "What does Little Me need right now?" When judgment rears its ugly head, tap into the curiosity that came easily as a child and watch your entire world transform.

> **Self-Trust:** As you embark on this journey, I encourage you to trust yourself above all else, even if you've never felt safe doing so. Trust the messages your body sends you when it hurts.

Trust your instincts if something on the trail or in your life sets off alarm bells. Trust your inner knowing about what is right for you at every moment. One way to practice this on the trail is to listen to your body when you feel like you need to use the restroom. When you gotta go, you gotta go, and finding a way to relieve yourself instead of holding it is one of the quickest ways to reestablish the trust you have in not only your body's signals but also your brain's capacity to take action.

Patience: This process isn't pretty. You're going to make mistakes, say things you don't mean, and probably lose some relationships along the way. I can't tell you how many times I've wished to go back to my prehealing days, blissfully ignorant of my pain and how it was impacting every facet of my life. You can't rush through this. You can't heal everything all at once, nor should you try. Settle in, double up on your patience, and commit to the journey. You're worth it.

MINDFUL MILES

The Mindful Miles section at the end of each chapter includes prompts that you can use to start connecting the dots on your own Trail of Life, and they can turn any activity into an opportunity for self-discovery, personal growth, and healing. When our brains get squirrelly on a seated meditation, we return to the breath. We utilize these prompts in the same way to ground ourselves on the trail. If you're out on a hike and you find yourself getting distracted by the physical sensations you're experiencing or the thoughts that come up, simply return to the prompts to refocus your attention. If you find your mind frequently wandering, or fixating on one thing, make note of any thoughts or sensations in your body. If your brain is busy like mine, flitting from thought to thought like a hummingbird, paying attention to every single one can feel exhausting, but stick with it.

Using Mindful Miles as a grounding practice for your hike will help you identify a couple things:

- If you're able to focus on the question, then you'll learn something about yourself.

- If you get distracted, making a note of which thought came up is another data point to consider. If this repeats itself, you'll have a record of it and can use this as an opportunity to dig deeper and ask yourself why it's coming up.

NEXT STEPS

If hiking helped me heal my mind and body from trauma and disease, then it can help you heal too. You can read books, go for hikes, and create time to connect the dots, but what happens next? How do you keep putting one foot in front of the other on the path to your dreams? The Next Steps section of each chapter offers a ritual, activity, or action item for you to complete to help you keep moving forward on your Trail of Life.

Finally, if at any point reading this book you find yourself feeling some type of way, I invite you to grab a piece of paper or your trusty journal, or even use the margins of this book, to jot it down. You can also simply sit and think about these questions:

- What am I feeling right now?

- Where do I feel it in my body?

- Can I remember the last time I felt this way? What caused the feeling then?

That's all. You don't have to wax poetic about the feeling, I'm not going to ask you to sit with the discomfort for too long, I simply want you to acknowledge what you feel and where you feel it.

At the end of the day, I'm just a gal who loves hiking and wants to help people come home to themselves. When I had access to a therapist, I was terrified of the stigma. When I was ready for therapy, I couldn't afford it. Everything shared in this book is something that helped me, and my hope is that it will help you too. If you come across a prompt or activity that doesn't resonate with you right now, permission is granted to skip it. As with anything in life, when it comes to the suggestions I'm sharing in this book, take what works for you and leave the rest.

So come sit next to me around the campfire. It's story time.

CHAPTER 1

YOU ONLY GET SO MANY SUNSETS

Unpacking Grief and Loss

The night before we set off on the Trans-Catalina Trail, I was nervous and struggling to fall asleep after one too many beers. I knew that the first day on the trail would be the hardest. I'd be hiking eleven to fifteen miles depending on which route we took, climbing up and down five peaks, carrying all of our food and the day's water for this adventure. My mind was racing, and I tossed and turned until I finally fell asleep. I woke up to my alarm, scrambled for my stuff in the dark, strapped on my backpack, and got in the elevator with Barry. I had never done this before, and I had no clue what we were up against, so in case we died on the first day, I wanted a selfie of us before we even got to the island.

"HERE WE GO!" I posted to Facebook.

We took the earliest ferry from Long Beach to get a bright and early start. The ride over to Avalon was a blur of excitement and nervous energy. I mentally reviewed the items in my backpack, making sure I hadn't forgotten anything. I had all the essentials and a few items that made Barry roll his eyes. (What do you mean "normal people don't bring a deck of tarot cards on a backpacking trip"?)

I was ready.

My Functional Anxiety Disguise: I'm smiling, but I'm actually terrified about what comes next.

By the time we arrived, the sleepy island town of Avalon was just starting to rise and shine. We checked in for the trail, got a map of the island, and began making our way toward the trailhead.

But walking through Avalon, we got turned around and started heading in the opposite direction of the trail. How were we supposed to find our way across this island if we couldn't even find the trailhead? When we realized our mistake, we stopped to get our bearings, found the trail, and followed a series of aggressive switchbacks that led us up and out of the canyon. As we gained elevation climbing up to the ridge-line, I could see a cruise ship on the horizon, waiting to pull into port.

Not even an hour into this adventure, I felt my right shoe rubbing against the outside of my heel, the beginning stages of a blister. Barry had described this as a *hot spot* when he was helping me prepare for the hike, and he'd advised me that if I felt this start to happen, we should stop hiking and tape it up, hopefully avoiding a blister altogether. When I started to feel this pain, I had a battle with my inner critic. *What will*

Barry think of me having a blister this early in the adventure? Does that mean I'm terrible at this? Should I turn around and wait in Avalon while he completes the trail? If I quit, will he still love me?

Eventually, I got tired of my own spiraling, so I stopped hiking and started looking for an area where I could take care of the blister. I didn't have a lot of practice standing up for myself or advocating for my needs, and on the rare occasions when I did, I would overexplain, feeling like I had to sell whoever I was with on why my needs were valid. For me to simply acknowledge the pain, stop hiking, and start taking care of myself was new, and I was delighted by how well Barry received this. There was no back talk, no poking fun at me, no jokes made about my already exhausted body—just love, understanding, and a desire to help.

Once we stopped, I looked around for a level place to put my pack, but I couldn't find one. I had visions of a Cheryl Strayed moment up there, sending my shoe over the side of the mountain down toward the cruise ship. Never one to miss an opportunity to one-up tragic thoughts, my imagination sent my backpack sailing after. Barry handed me the roll of Leukotape and walked me through how to tape up the affected area. It felt better when I put my socks and shoes back on, and we continued hiking.

Everything was steep. Everything was hurting. I was having a hard time catching my breath during the tough climb out of the canyon. It was December, but it felt like July. While the temperature never rose above seventy-five degrees, there was no coverage or shade on the trail, only full sun. I was struggling physically, feeling other hot spots develop on both feet. My toes felt cramped and crushed in my shoes. *When will these switchbacks end? Does this trail ever flatten out, or is the entire hike going to be an uphill climb, kicking up dust and sending waves of heat rising from the ground?* It felt like I had opened the oven door and stuck my face into the blast of hot air. I couldn't help but laugh at myself and my lack of preparation, as evidenced by my blister. *Apparently wearing hiking boots at your standing desk isn't the same as breaking them in, Sydney.*

As if he were inside my head, hearing my self-doubt, Barry would occasionally turn around and shout back to me, "Proud of you!" and snap me out of whatever negative loop I was stuck in.

The first time he said it, it made me cry. Truth be told, I didn't know if I could do it. I didn't know if we'd make it to the end in one piece, but I knew I wanted to try. At that point, simply *wanting* to try felt like a victory. Prior to taping up the blister, all I could focus on was how much the experience had sucked so far. In the first three miles of the thirty-eight-and-a-half-mile adventure, the weight of the life I'd lived so far was starting to take its toll on me. I was the heaviest I'd ever been, and I hadn't trained at all. Plus, I was carrying close to thirty-five pounds of gear on my back, which only compounded the pain.

We continued up to the ridgeline, where the steep, single-track trail leveled out and opened up to a wide dirt road. That was the first time I was consciously aware of how my energy, anxious thoughts, and pain leveled out and opened up as well, my inner wilderness matching the rugged wilderness I was moving through on the island. That awareness gave me an opportunity to slow my breathing, allow my strides to lengthen, and settle in to that section of the trail. In the absence of the glaring physical difficulty of climbing, I was able to be present to the world around me and within me. Having just overcome my first battle on the trail—a blister and a gnarly climb—I began to understand that the weight I was carrying wasn't only in my physical body and strapped to my back. I was also wearing an invisible backpack—which I'd later come to call my trauma pack—that was weighing me down even further.

As I mentioned before, the two years leading up to the hike were some of the most difficult years of my life.

First, Chris had died. We'd met Chris when I was working at a sky-diving center running events, PR, and marketing. I was also a member of a competitive skydiving team affiliated with the center. Barry ran the skydiving school. Chris came in one day—early forties, slender build, kind eyes, and a smile that would lift the energy of any person or animal in his proximity. Chris was a legendary bodysurfer in Newport Beach and an army veteran who'd traveled around the world, including multiple tours through Iran and Iraq, before receiving an honorable discharge. Chris had earned his jump wings in the army, but he still had to go through the progression with Barry to earn his civilian skydiving license. We all became fast friends.

The Chris I knew would make me laugh so hard I cried. He was one of the brightest lights in our lives at the time, and the fact that he'd taken his own life had me perplexed. Later I found out more about the kinds of battles he'd been facing.

I learned that Chris had applied for mental health benefits with the Department of Veterans Affairs (VA), and the process was brutal. He was going to the VA often, sometimes multiple times per week, trying to get help. He finally discovered he had fibromyalgia, brought on by post-traumatic stress disorder (PTSD). He'd been having violent night-mares, and in January he started undergoing sleep tests.

Before his death, Chris decided to file for disability with the VA for PTSD. If accepted, they would pay for his medical care for the rest of his life. The filing process required that he outline every excruciating detail of every event during his military career that might have con-tributed to his PTSD.

Just two days after filling out those forms, Chris took his own life.

After Barry broke the news to me, I went to the skydiving center. I walked past my boss, and he asked me what was wrong.

"Chris killed himself last night," I said through tears, still shocked by the words as they crossed my lips. Now it was real.

"Why are you so upset?" he asked. "It's not like you knew him for very long. Suicide is selfish, anyway." He strode off, leaving me in a puddle of my own tears.

Later he told me that if I went to Chris's memorial instead of going to a planned training camp with my skydiving team, it would be a disservice to our training plan and an inconvenience to my teammates. At that point, I was still a world-class people pleaser and an expert at sacrificing my needs to avoid conflict, so I opted to train instead of going to the memorial.

Five months later, my Uncle Mike died from brain cancer. My uncle was a gay man, a singer, an actor, an entrepreneur, a designer, a creator, and the personification of love. One of my most vivid memories of him was when he told me about Burning Man. He and his creative cohorts had a camp there for years, and when he showed me photos from one of his art installations, I thought they were fake. No way there was that much art—and that many people dressed in creative costumes—in the middle of the desert. Growing up in the suburbs of Kansas City, I hadn't seen deserts before. I didn't know that Burning Man was real. I just thought my uncle liked dressing up and digitally manipulating pictures.

When he was diagnosed with brain cancer, his doctors gave him a couple of years to live, tops. The treatments and the tumor itself had impacted his speaking and singing voice, and it was heartbreaking to hear him try to find the words that had so effortlessly floated from his lips for decades prior. When Uncle Mike's memorial was planned in Kansas, I had a tough choice to make. All of my money was going to rent, student loans, food, insurance, and team training. I had none left over for travel, so I passed on the opportunity to celebrate my uncle's life.

Just three months after Uncle Mike died, I woke up one day ahead of my alarm and started scrolling mindlessly through Facebook. I saw that my friend Eric had changed his Facebook picture to a photo of him and my friend Adam. Another friend had posted a photo on Adam's wall.

All of the hair stood up on the back of my neck, and I started to panic. In the skydiving community, when people died, everyone changed their Facebook profile photo to a black square to indicate that someone close to them had died. Eric's wasn't a black square, but given that Adam was away on a BASE jumping trip, my anxious brain assumed the worst. I texted Adam, but he didn't reply.

Our most recent messages were from just three days before. He'd been asking how many jumps he could make in a day, since he needed to do a certain number in a specific window and was trying to figure out where he could get the most jumps in—either at the skydiving center where I worked or somewhere else. I'd responded, but I was short. I didn't ask him what the goal was. I just gave him the answer he was looking for.

Adam, like Chris, was another one of Barry's Kidz, our nickname for the folks who learned to skydive under Barry's supervision. Adam had learned in eight days. When we moved from Chicago to Southern California in late 2011, Adam wasn't far behind. He moved to California as well and even lived with us for a bit.

I didn't hear any more news about Adam until later that day when my phone rang. It was Eric.

"Is Adam okay?" I asked, praying it was a yes, but feeling deep in my soul that it was a no.

I don't remember exactly what Eric said, but I ran out of that office wailing.

Adam was early in his BASE jumping career, and he'd been doing bridge jumps with no problems. On that particular day, he was jumping from a cliff. When he deployed his parachute, it opened wrong, turning him away from his desired flight path and back toward the cliff face. He struck the cliff he'd jumped from, falling some two hundred feet after the initial impact. One of the people he was jumping with administered CPR while they waited for the medics, but the medics were unable to evacuate him before he died.

I tried to work that day. I tried to do anything other than cry.

Eventually my boss at the skydiving center, who was also my skydiving coach, a member of my skydiving team, and our personal friend, heard what had happened to Adam.

"Well, that's a choice he made," he said callously, "to jump off that cliff."

There was no acknowledgment that someone I considered a little brother had just died. There was no consideration for my feelings.

I took the rest of the day off, went to the liquor store, and got all the supplies we'd need to engage in our favorite coping mechanism—drinking our feelings. We would share stories about Adam, trying to make sense of what happened. I looked at my bank account. I only had enough money to get to either the USPA National Skydiving Championships *or* Adam's funeral. Both would be in Illinois, and we couldn't afford two trips. I had a choice to make, and after skipping the memorials for Chris and my uncle, I knew what I was going to do. My boss feigned understanding when I informed him that I'd be skipping nationals to go to Adam's memorial, and within the week they found someone to replace me on the team. I didn't know it at the time, but the choice to go to Adam's memorial rather than nationals was the first domino to fall in my career in the skydiving industry.

A few months after Adam's funeral, I woke up to a text message from a friend. It was a screenshot of a Facebook comment accusing my boss of raping a minor. I went straight into detective mode and hopped onto the county court website to see if I could find his arrest record. It didn't take me long. My stomach sank into my toes as I read the words on my phone. Multiple felony charges. Preventing the victim from reporting. Unlawful sex with a minor. Lewd and lascivious acts with a minor under fourteen, with force. Oral copulation with a person under sixteen. Penetration with a person under eighteen. My vision started crossing, and I felt like I was going to throw up.

The queasiness in my stomach soon gave way to rage. Barry and I had moved from rural Illinois to Southern California so I could train with my boss, in the hopes of becoming a world champion skydiver someday. He'd been instrumental in helping me change my mindset, overcome my fears, and tap into my peak levels of performance. I'd trusted him with my life in the sky. Plus, he signed my paychecks, and he'd been so helpful in ensuring that Barry and I felt connected to the community. How could he jeopardize everything we'd been working so hard for together, let alone *his* entire life, career, and legacy?

That accusation removed my blinders and put a spotlight on issues I'd been overlooking. Between the comments about Chris and Adam and other difficulties with the business and our skydiving team, our relationship had deteriorated, and we were barely speaking to each other. He was short with me, and I just wanted to do my job.

Given all the losses I was still grieving, I decided to take a break from jumping when Adam died. My boss wasn't happy about it. He was so dismissive of my experiences that it felt like it didn't matter what kind of state I was in mentally or emotionally. As a result, I began to question how long it was taking me to grieve. *Should I be ready to jump by now? Am I a weak competitor for allowing these losses to impact me in this way?*

I was also worried about my job. I didn't want to be responsible for cleaning things up if the news that one of the owners of the skydiving center had been accused of sexually assaulting a minor blew back on the business. If the accusation were true, and I had a feeling it was, I couldn't continue generating revenue for the business to line the pockets of a sexual predator. That wasn't how my legacy in the sport was going to play out.

At an all-staff meeting, my boss walked around telling everyone that we shouldn't worry. What had happened was consensual. His business partner defended him, saying the victim was making it all up.

Which one was it? Was it consensual, or was the victim lying? The stories weren't lining up, and I knew things were going to get messy.

It was all too much. I didn't have any fight left in me. During the four years I was a skydiver, twenty-three of my friends had died. Three were veteran suicides, one died in a motorcycle accident, and the remaining nineteen died while skydiving or BASE jumping. I didn't want to start over with a new skydiving team or coach. I didn't want to move to another skydiving center and try to get a new job. It was hands down the best skydiving center in the industry, and I clearly wasn't having fun working there anymore. I'd also made too many sacrifices already to support my skydiving dreams, not least missing Chris's and my uncle's memorials.

My last day of work was December 29, 2014. That date also marks my final skydive. After nearly seven hundred jumps in four years, I walked away from my hopes of becoming a world champion skydiver, my dream job, and the sport that had introduced me to the love of my life.

TRAIL OF LIFE

I know this is a really depressing start to our journey together in this book, but I'm hoping that as I share some of the items that have been weighing down my invisible backpack, you'll feel a little less alone. I don't know about you, but we didn't really talk about grief in my house—whether that was grieving the end of a job, the end of a relationship, or the loss of a pet or a loved one. My father had a tendency to use humor as his default coping mechanism, and my mother buried herself in books or otherwise avoided difficult conversations, so learning how to sit with my discomfort, process grief, and soothe myself was never modeled for me. When all these people I cared about started dying in rapid succession, I was in over my head. I didn't have any tools to draw on, other than drinking to excess and finding comfort in a pint of ice cream.

At this point in my life though, my best advice to everyone suffering grief or loss is this: Get help; treat the wound!

We are all conditioned to prioritize physical pain over emotional pain. A perfect example of this was when I tended to my blister on that first day's hike far more promptly than I'd ever tended to the emotions swirling through my head. But physical trauma isn't the only kind of trauma. Trauma isn't a scratch. It's an open wound.

If I were next to you while you were reading this, and I had a compound fracture of my arm—with the bone sticking out of the skin—you'd put down the book and get help. Maybe you'd even take me to the hospital. When we arrived at the hospital, we'd see an X-ray of the damage done. When we got the cast, we'd be able to touch the solution that would help heal that damage. We might be frustrated that we'd be tending to an injury for weeks or months, but at least we'd understand that the bone was broken and needed more time to heal.

But we don't do that with emotional trauma.

How often do we see someone on the street in a mental health crisis and keep walking? How many times have we experienced feelings of anxiety or depression and felt completely alone because nobody could see our wounds?

Instead of offering help, we tell folks to suck it up.

"Don't cry."

We have an unrealistic expectation of the time it takes to properly grieve, so we succumb to unhealthy coping mechanisms or rush back to life, love, and work, assuming if we're busy enough we can outrun the pain.

When we avoid our emotional breaking points, our bodies take the brunt of it. That was certainly the case for me. My first reaction when Adam died was to go with what I knew—drinking to forget the pain. I was drinking to the point of blacking out before his death, and I kept drinking that way for years after. It was easier to open a bottle of wine and numb out in front of the television than it was to sit with my discomfort.

Much like how we should treat emotional trauma with the same tenacity we do physical trauma, we should also hold space for all kinds of grief. People dying isn't the only kind of loss that we grieve. Perhaps you're grieving after a breakup, a divorce, the establishment of a boundary, the end of a friendship, the loss of a pet, or the death of a dream. All of these are important. All of these require grieving.

MINDFUL MILES

Regardless of where you are in the grief cycle, regardless of what memories come up for you, I want you to know that you can do this. If it's not today, that's fine. If it's not tomorrow, that's okay too. This is *your* healing journey. You have the agency to determine when the right time is for you to move through this pain. If you're ready, let's get started:

- What tools do you have in your toolbox to process grief?

- Is there anything in your trauma pack that you've been avoiding?

- Who have you lost in your life, and what is your favorite memory of them?

NEXT STEPS

At the end of a long day of jumping out of airplanes, Adam always encouraged us to stop what we were doing and catch the sunset. Every single time he'd say, "You only get so many sunsets." Whether the sky was ablaze in a swirl of pinks and purples or a complete shutout, we savored each one. It's one of my favorite memories with him, and whenever I'm hosting a retreat, I build in time to enjoy the sunset as a group and share this story.

When you're ready, I invite you to create a day of remembrance for a person or pet you've lost, using this chapter's prompts. Far too often we have unrealistic expectations of how quickly we should move through our grief, and unless we come from a culture with defined traditions around grief, particularly the end of life, we may feel clueless as to how to start. Through this activity, you can create your own process that feels good to you.

First, find a hike you'd like to do. For situations like this, I recommend a trail you've traveled before, so you aren't caught up in where you're going and can settle in with your thoughts in a familiar environment. If the person you're remembering was one of your adventure buddies, consider returning to a place you enjoyed together. Gather some photos, old clothing, or something you can hold in your hands that reminds you of this person. I know it can be painful to remember the good times with the people we've lost, but allow yourself to imagine what it would be like if the roles were reversed. If, after you die, someone you love is missing you, wouldn't you want them to remember the good times you shared more than the pain of your absence?

After your hike, do something that reminds you of the people you've lost. When I was living in San Diego and I was missing Adam, I would grab his favorite sandwich and head out to Sunset Cliffs to watch the sunset. Think of the good times you shared, look through old pictures, and allow the joy you experienced with this person to wash over your entire body. The people who love us who are no longer with us don't want us to be stuck in our sadness. They want us to live full, happy, healthy lives. After you've had your day of remembrance, find someone to share your stories and memories with. Whether that person is a shared connection or a total stranger, it's through sharing memories that we can rekindle the connection we had with our loved ones who are gone and keep their legacies alive.

CHAPTER 2

FROM THE BOTTOM TO THE TOP

Trying Something New

When we found the Trans-Catalina Trail, I wasn't even remotely outdoorsy, but I already had big dreams of being a long-distance back-packer. Despite having zero experience, I had set a goal to be a Triple Crown thru-hiker—someone who has hiked the Pacific Crest Trail (which extends from Mexico to Canada, traveling through California, Oregon, and Washington), the Appalachian Trail (which extends from Georgia to Maine, through the Appalachian Mountains), and the Continental Divide Trail (which follows the Rocky Mountains through five states from Mexico to Canada).

I thought hiking across Catalina Island could be a good trip to test the waters before committing to an adventure that would require me to leave life behind for six months. While the thirty-eight and a half miles of the TCT are remote, you're never days away from getting help like you are on the longer national scenic trails. And while we'd opted to carry all our food for the journey, there was also food available in Avalon, at the island's airport restaurant at mile thirteen, and in Two Harbors, so we could have lightened our load if we had wanted to. Also, every campground had water available—the first three had running water, and the last, Parsons Landing, would deliver water to you in a locker. All of those amenities took a lot of the challenging parts out of backpacking and left me with some basic things to evaluate: Will I like being out there for days on end? Can I sleep well on the trail? How will my body respond to longer hikes? How much food and water will I need each day to sustain my energy? Hiking across the island wasn't the same kind of commitment as some of the longer thru-hiking routes, but I was curious how it would feel to hike from one end of the island to the other. I was anticipating feeling mighty and victorious, a triumphant sense of accomplishment.

I knew it wasn't going to be easy, but the hike had been brutal so far and we were only part way through day one. We were at mile three at the first shade structure, and I already had blisters forming. I was parched and sucked down water while taking in the scenery around me. As I took some deep breaths to try to slow my heart rate, I noticed the air smelled sweeter at that elevation.

In the videos we watched from other folks who had done the trail, we noticed that there was a playground in the middle of the backcountry, and they were saying it was about the halfway point for the first day. I looked at the map as we started to pack up to keep going, evaluating how my body felt. The playground was near mile six, and our first campground was between miles ten and eleven. As we made our way farther into the interior of the island, Barry and I noticed the landscape had shifted a bit. We alternated between dirt roads and a single track, sometimes with 360-degree ocean views. Even though my feet were killing me, the wilderness that surrounded us was so beautiful it was almost enough to make me forget about the pain.

We reached a place that was perfect for photos, with a water view, and I raised my hands in the air for the first full-body photo I had taken in a long time. As we left the spot, we started to descend into a canyon, and I was thankful for the break from climbing.

I started daydreaming about what the next day would bring as we walked past fields of sage plants, each level step a welcome respite for my aching legs. The section from Black Jack Campground to Little Harbor was primarily downhill after we passed the airport. Hiking downhill felt so good after miles of uphill climbing to get to the ridgeline. I imagined the most luxurious cruise into our second campground, and an even more relaxing day off in Little Harbor the day after.

As I lifted my head out of my downhill daydream, I noticed a glint of light reflecting on something ahead of us. It was a slide! Next to it I could make out a swing set, and were those monkey bars? The YouTubers weren't kidding; it was a full-on playground in the middle of the backcountry.

As we came up closer to the playground, I started thinking of ways I could extend our break there and delay our return to the trail. I was in the most pain I had experienced in recent memory, and I couldn't stop sweating. At that point we were six miles in, and I hadn't done a hike longer than that since we first moved to California five years prior. I knew Barry would love me regardless of my performance on the trip, but I didn't want to leave anything to chance. I really wanted to be good at hiking.

I've completed nearly seven hundred skydives, but asking for this full-body photo was scarier than any of them.

In fact, I've always wanted to be good at everything. When I was a competitive skydiver, I developed my skills quickly. I won medals in local and regional competitions and went to the USPA National Skydiving Championships just three years into my career as a skydiver. Excellence was my standard, but that had been a challenging standard to maintain in the last few years. I'd been tussling with a lot of questions.

After leaving my dream job and walking away from my goal of being a world champion skydiver, I had some unfinished business and something to prove to myself. Was I actually good at creating events or had I been riding the coattails of a sexual predator and a prestigious skydiving center? Could I sell out events that I created by myself? What kind of events would I want to go to if I were still interested in jumping out of planes?

I created a skydiving events company called Planet Green Socks, named after the green socks that Adam wore on his skydives and BASE jumps, and a nod to our shared desire to travel around the world. I stayed on the ground—no more jumps for me—but I created skills camps for experienced skydivers in Southern California and brought in some of the best athletes in the sport to lead the camps. Every event we created sold out, and everyone had an incredible time. But I was still unhappy. It didn't matter whether I was doing events on my own or for a big skydiving center; it wasn't my passion anymore.

The last event I hosted in skydiving was Adam's memorial event. It occurred in May, eight months after Adam died. It was an incredibly emotional experience, and as his fellow teammates and friends released his ashes into the sky, I knew my time in the sport was over. I wouldn't say it was the perfect way to end my time in skydiving, but it felt like a nice bow on a beautiful, if not tragic, chapter of my life.

A few months after Adam's memorial, Barry lost his job and his dream. He had been a professional skydiver for sixteen years at that point and it ended in a proverbial dumpster fire at the skydiving center where we'd both worked. There was a lot of drama in the aftermath of my old boss being convicted on two of the felony counts, and my husband got caught in the crosshairs of a failing business. The months that followed were brutal, and we both started drinking heavily. I was looking for answers to life's problems in the bottom of a bottle of a wine or a pint of Ben & Jerry's, and I was eating everything in sight.

Despite the difficulty of navigating so much at once, all of these changes gave me an opportunity to reflect and refocus my energy and efforts. Barry and I hit the road with our dogs and set out to explore some of California before we made our next moves. From Joshua Tree National Park to Big Sur, through the Bay Area, and back down to Southern California, I kept asking myself these questions: What did I want to do with my time and talent? Where did I want to live? What did my dream day look like?

I wanted stability. A good paycheck and benefits package. A smart team to work with. Big clients like I had when I worked in a PR and marketing agency. I wanted to be back in agency land. I wanted to feel useful and professional and confident in my skills again. On the way back home from our road trip, I spoke with my mentor, Aaron, who was working at the agency I left when I decided to skydive full-time. I shared that I had retired from skydiving entirely and taken time to myself to figure out what I wanted, and I asked if there were any opportunities at the agency.

In late 2015, I ended up going back to the agency as a contractor. At the time, jumping back into corporate work felt incredible. The pace was fast, and I was refreshed, ready to take on everything that could possibly come my way. The familiarity of long hours, a demanding workload, and praise from clients and colleagues was intoxicating. Looking back, working around the clock with no time for myself felt incredible, because it was easier to throw myself back into the chaos of my corporate career than it was to sit with my feelings and process the grief of losing twenty-three friends in four years.

When we moved to San Diego the following year, it was a clean slate. I paid off my debt from when I was training and started making a bigger dent in my student loans. My parents were stoked that I wasn't jumping out of planes anymore. Compared to the measly wage I was being paid while I worked in skydiving, I had a big paycheck, cushy benefits, and I was launching a new wine brand and working with Fortune 500 companies like Intel, Comcast, and NBCUniversal—household names that made for good bragging rights. Everything in my life looked like it was turning around. I was finally able to relax and breathe a little. I was *adulting.*

TRAIL OF LIFE

That was all new, and in the spirit of trying something else new, I agreed to go on a backpacking trip with Barry. He was an experienced outdoorsman, but I needed something that was a good entry-level distance for someone who hadn't done more than one day of hiking in a row. If it was local to Southern California, even better. I remembered Adam telling me about his desire to hike the Pacific Crest Trail, and even though I was nervous, I had started getting excited about doing a shorter version of a long-distance hike.

So there we were on the Trans-Catalina Trail, and I was quickly (and humbly) discovering that, despite my quest for excellence, I was right back on the bottom rung again. I was a beginner. In the past, being new at something was a source of frustration because I felt guilty if I wasn't immediately proficient at it. Through my experiences in skydiving, I learned how to reflect on each training jump I did, which helped me embrace my newbie status, and grew to love the feeling of learning something new, regardless of how I performed. Somewhere along the way through all the grief and loss, I had forgotten how invigorated I felt when learning something new.

After that first day on the TCT, I adopted a new mantra for myself: I give myself permission to learn at my own pace. To translate that into hiking terms, I committed to hiking my own hike—moving at my own pace, resting and taking breaks when I needed to, and ultimately doing it in a way that was sustainable for me. Despite the hike being the most difficult thing I'd ever attempted for the sheer physicality of it, it was reminding me of how much I loved learning, and I was grateful for the perspective shift.

Have you ever started a completely new activity, job, hobby, or relationship and had wild expectations of instant success or proficiency? I know I have, and when we take a step back and consider the world we're living in, it makes sense. In American culture, we are really quick to celebrate folks who have reached the top of their chosen profession or activity. Our society celebrates success, then dissects the path taken to get there. When we try to replicate someone else's Trail of Life for ourselves, we end up mimicking the steps that led to the success without ever stopping to consider if the steps they took are the right steps for us. Our brains are wired to identify patterns and keep us safe, so it makes sense that we would try to replicate what has already worked for someone else. The problem is, success is very rarely about the specific steps taken, and has everything to do with our capacity to keep moving forward when the going gets tough. When we focus on the how (the steps taken) instead of the why (the motivation to keep going) behind the what (the success),

Is there anything better than a sudden breeze on a hot hike? I hope you can feel this picture.

we rob ourselves of a beautiful experience. As Barry would say, when we're so focused on traveling the path that has worked for others, we may be blind to the zip line that can get us to our destination.

MINDFUL MILES

As we get older, it can be scary to try something new, but if you're reading this book, you've survived every first time so far in your life. And if you're at all like me, you probably have a list a mile long of things you'd like to try, but for whatever reason haven't tried yet. These prompts are helpful whether you're feeling nostalgic about how you used to try new things without fear, or you're feeling stuck and need a nudge to help you get warmed up to the idea of trying something new.

- When was the last time you tried something for the first time?

- How did you feel before you did it?

- How did it feel to do it?

- How do you feel about that experience now?

NEXT STEPS

What do you want to learn more about or try in the next year? Do you want to learn a new language? Try an improv class? Spend more time in meditation, journaling, or moving your body? Make a list of the things you've always wanted to try, but for whatever reason you haven't done yet. If you're like me and find checking boxes on a list extremely satisfying, turn this into a bucket list and make the timing specific, like "Forty things I want to try before my fortieth birthday."

If you don't have a lot of practice trying new things, pick the low-hanging fruit on the list first to build your confidence. Start with the activities that are free or easily accessible to you right now and go for it! When we're able to check boxes easily and consistently, it can help us build momentum to start tackling the bigger items on the list and help us remember how capable we are.

When I was a competitive skydiver, I tried new things on every training jump. During our first training camp as a team, we got down from each jump and met in our team room to debrief the video. As soon as I saw my first error, I started giving a real-time commentary about how much I was screwing up. I had a list a mile long of mistakes I made. My coach paused the video and stopped me in my tracks. He had given us a framework to use to debrief—watch the video in its entirety in silence, then one by one, we'd go around the circle and debrief ourselves:

- Name three things that went well.

- Name three things I'd like to improve on.

- List how I would improve those things, and if I didn't have a solution, that's what my coach was for; he'd help me navigate how to correct the mistakes.

Sometimes I really screwed up, and the only thing that went well on a skydive was the fact that my parachute opened on time and I landed safely, but we always started by looking for positives first. This was a huge mindset shift for me, and it took a ton of practice before seeing the positives first came naturally. These days, I might not always jump to the positives first but on the rare occasion that I don't, I catch myself quickly and can interrupt a shame spiral of things I need to improve with a few positives. In the sky, on the ground, in my relationships, in my work—this is a superpower.

As you start trying new things, you might find that you fall into the same patterns I did at the beginning of my competitive skydiving career. If you do, carve out some time to deepen your self-reflection practice and debrief the experience by following the steps outlined above.

CHAPTER 3

GIRL, HOW DID WE GET HERE?

Unpacking Body Image

Once I'd decided to give the backpacking thing a try and embark on the Trans-Catalina Trail, I started making a list of gear that I needed for my debut voyage. After doing a bunch of research, I wanted to go somewhere I could try everything on, see how it fit, and feel confident in what I was purchasing before investing a significant amount of money. And with that, we made our way to the Encinitas REI store.

I headed straight to the hiking apparel section and found a shirt and a pair of pants I liked. I grabbed the sizes I usually wore and scurried off to the dressing room.

Hiking! We're doing this! I thought.

I yanked my pants down, tore off my shirt.

I'm going to hike across Catalina Island!

I took the pants off the hanger and slid the moisture-wicking fabric over my right leg.

Oooh, these are niiiice! I thought as I pulled on the other pant leg.

Uh-oh. I couldn't pull the pants all the way up, and there was exactly a 0 percent chance that I'd be able to button them if I did.

Maybe outdoor gear is sized differently.

I took off the tight pants and put my own pants back on. As I was pulling up my flowy pants with an elastic waistband, I had a flashback to the first time I remembered caring about clothing sizes. It was so vivid that I felt like I was time traveling and was transported to my freshman-year body, back in the locker room, trying on my cheerleading uniform.

The memory was of walking through the halls after school, making my way to cheerleading practice. I had been so excited. Today was uniform-fitting day. I did it! After years of cheering for Pop Warner football, taking gymnastics classes, and practicing very hard, I was a high school cheerleader. One of the reasons I was so excited was simply the uniform itself. The high school uniforms had sparkly metallic gold accents instead of the mustard yellow accents that we had on our uniforms when we cheered for Pop Warner football as kids. Now we were bright and shiny and sparkly. Our poms had metallic gold in them too. No more of that trash-bag material; these were real poms.

The uniform-fitting days were set up like an assembly line, with all the uniform components stacked in piles by size. The first size I tried was too small. My coach gave an eye roll and looked exasperated when I came back for a bigger size. I remember her handing me a size nine skirt, and I started comparing. The other girls were wearing smaller sizes, much smaller. My world wasn't shattered, I didn't have some Hollywood-worthy meltdown, but standing in front of the mirror in my size nine skirt, I pulled my signature get-smaller move. I stood on my tiptoes and sucked in, holding my breath, seeing what I would look like if I were thinner. Like many moments over the course of my life, I saw my thinner body and longed to appear smaller. I had locked in my mission: Get a hot body. Be smaller.

Now there I was, thirty-one years old, staring at myself in a dressing room mirror and still struggling to get a too-small garment on. I sheepishly hung up the pants that wouldn't fit and went back out to the rack. I looked at the largest size they had, a sixteen. Knowing I couldn't even get the size twelve over my hips, I reluctantly grabbed the sixteen, passing over size fourteen, each size tag screaming at me like a judgment: "Keep moving, fatty, and don't collect $200."

The enthusiasm that had had me inflated, light, floating around the REI store, was now seeping out of my body, leaking like air out of a balloon. I pulled the door closed behind me and took a deep breath.

I took off my comfy pants again, and I held my breath as I shimmied into the bigger size. They were tighter than I thought they would be, and that was the largest size available. No other brands at the store made pants bigger than these. I wanted hiking pants, not some bullshit knockoff brand or poorly made pair of pants from a store that sells larger sizes. As I sat down, the waistband dug into my midsection. I stood up, looked at the length of the pants, and shook my head. Apparently all women who are a size sixteen are also professional basketball players, because these pants were too long for my five-foot-four frame. I stood up on my tippy-toes and sucked in. I started to wonder if the dressing room was a time machine, because I was thrust back into the past again. This time it was a conversation with my mother.

My mother once said to me, "Sydney, you'd better watch what you eat, because if you don't, you'll end up like me."

I was young and I didn't understand. *What does she mean? I'll end up being a cool cheer mom? I'll give the shirt off my back for someone in need? Why is that bad and what does that have to do with the food I eat?*

My mother is fat and has been since she had babies and stopped smoking cigarettes. As a family, we were always trying some new diet: Atkins, WeightWatchers, low-fat everything. Growing up, I observed how my mother picked herself apart in the mirror and how poorly she spoke about her body. It was never explicitly taught or said, but my young mind came to understand that in that house, bigger bodies were bad and smaller bodies were good. As I grew up, my friends and society in general—media, books, music, movies, and TV shows—all confirmed my suspicions.

I know now that my mother meant well when she told me that, but back then all it did was instill fear in me and confirm that being fat would be my biggest offense as a woman in our society, regardless of how good of a person I was, what I achieved, or who I was in community with. Throughout my life, even when I was fit and healthy, I felt the need to be smaller, with a body like a Victoria's Secret model and hair like you see in an Herbal Essences commercial.

When she said that to me, I was already addicted to earning gold stars. I didn't want her to think I was stupid by asking questions, so I nodded and made a note to always watch what I eat so I wouldn't end up fat like my mother.

Back in the dressing room, I slid the XL shirt off the hanger, also the biggest size they carried in the store, and squeezed the buttons together around my belly button. The shirt had buttons that snapped, and I didn't know how to feel about that. I imagined a button popping off on-trail, taking out one of Barry's eyes, leaving us stranded, down one eye in the backcountry because I was too fat for that shirt. So I guessed it was better that the shirt had snaps so we didn't have a button blowout. But then I worried about my shirt just ripping open like tearaway pants, my exposed body sending a shockwave in every direction, wiping out any and all plants, animals, and human beings in its wake.

That's how things go for me. That's how my brain works.

"Prepare for the worst, expect the best" has taught me to always identify and prepare for the absolute worst-case scenario before even considering that something could be normal, or okay, or maybe even terrific.

I snapped out of my shame spiral. After all, everything I'd read said that was the style of shirt I wanted. I didn't want cotton for a backpacking trip; I needed something that would dry quickly and protect me from the sun.

Feeling a bit like a sausage about to split its casing in my new attire, I paused and looked at myself in the mirror. Typically for me, going shopping includes a lot of self-judgment. I'll pick and poke at the parts of my body that I desperately want to fix while saying unkind things to myself about myself, just like my mother modeled for me. The train of thought about the button was exhausting. I let out a sigh and started to disrobe when I recalled something someone once said along the lines of, "If you wouldn't dream of saying it to your best friend, don't say it to yourself." It was in that dressing room that I committed to being my own best friend. I shrugged at myself in the mirror, continuing the conversation I was having in my head. I pretended that I was talking to my best friend in the mirror. She would never be on the receiving end of the terrible things I say to myself, or the worst-case scenarios I prepare for. No way, no how. I thought of how I'd start a conversation with my best friend, and we always start with an emphatic "girl."

"Girl," I said to myself, leaning all my weight on my left hip, gesturing wildly at a body I didn't recognize, "how did we get here?"

It was a rhetorical question, of course, but as I scanned my body head to toe, I started to connect the dots. My hair was the longest it had ever been. I had straightened it stick straight and kept up on my highlights, inching closer and closer to the type of woman I always envisioned I would be—fit, blonde, living near the beach in California. Short of having the perfect body, I checked off some of the success boxes I had achieved thus far: long blonde hair, great job with a great salary, living in SoCal, married to the man of my dreams, and living in the perfect house in San Diego. As I was standing in that dressing room in Encinitas, California, I gave younger me a shout-out. Little Sydney, the girl who grew up in Kansas watching *The O.C.* and *The Hills*, was getting ready for her first backpacking trip. We had been living in Southern California for five years, and the part of me that aspired to be like the girls on *The O.C.* felt mildly satisfied.

When I get thin, I'll have it all.

I flexed my muscles in the mirror, not because I had any, but because I wanted to stress test the shirt. It was a bit tight, and I didn't want to hulk out of it on the trail like I had with one of my shirts at a concert the year prior. So I did my best Arnold Schwarzenegger poses, and the material was surprisingly forgiving, even a bit stretchy.

I did some squats in the pants, stepped up on the bench to replicate taking big steps up on the trail, making sure I didn't split them open or pop a button. Again, pretty stretchy, pretty forgiving.

My stretching and flexing and stepping had me breathless in the dressing room. I moved closer to the mirror, almost bopping my own nose on the glass, staring into my own eyes. I took a deep breath, and instead of judging myself for working up a sweat trying on clothes, I half asked, half told myself, "What would be possible if we honored our inner athlete? From here on out, with the hike and beyond, could we try that?"

I nodded at myself in the mirror. I did another scan of my body and didn't judge it, just observed. As I took off the biggest sizes I had ever tried on and slid back into the comfortable clothes I'd arrived in, I felt a bit lighter. I had a bit more pep in my step after I left that store.

TRAIL OF LIFE

I want to note that *fat* is not a bad word. When I say, "My mother is fat and has been since she had babies and stopped smoking cigarettes," I'm not insulting her. I'm offering a descriptive word to help illustrate my point. Fat activists and leaders of the body positive movement all over the world are working hard to reclaim this word. When we reclaim the word, we reclaim our power. After a lifetime of hearing this word weaponized in our society, doing this takes a tremendous amount of awareness, discipline, and reframing to move through, so give yourself a lot of grace, and be patient with your progress.

In my own unpacking of my fear of being fat, I came to realize just how much negative power those three letters had held over my entire existence. It is wild to think back on how much energy I expended to try to stay small in order to avoid the pain and shame that follows this word. Between the warning from my mother, the lack of positive representation in the media I consumed, and the insults hurled at me throughout my life, it was pervasive. I was not only scared of being fat, I was convinced that if I allowed myself to get to that place, that I was also lazy, unattractive, and a stain on society. That is a lot to wrap your head around later in life with a fully developed brain, and even more damaging when we're figuring out our sense of self as we grow up. Prior to hiking the trail, one of my skydiving coaches told me I needed to weigh under 130 pounds if I ever had a dream of competing at an elite level. In addition to all of the self-worth issues that come with being a certain size in this society, my weight felt like a barrier to my success as an athlete. For so long, I had been dumbing myself down and denying my brilliance because a *smart* fat girl is a threat to the system. More specifically, I was always trying to create a smaller body to fit into. For as long as I could remember, I had been nitpicky about my body, uncomfortable in my own skin.

Already in the months leading up to the trip I had turned a corner. Instead of mindlessly scrolling and having a passive experience, I started to use social media intentionally. I stopped following accounts that made me feel bad about myself. I followed accounts that featured beautiful outdoor photography and inspired my adventurous spirit. I unfollowed brands that only showed me a thin, white standard of beauty and started seeking out body positive accounts, activists who celebrated women of all shapes, all races, all abilities. As the visuals in my feed diversified, so did my opinions of myself. As I saw more and more women posting their favorite pictures of themselves, feeling themselves, rocking the world in ways only they knew how, I widened my own definition of beauty. When I saw how many different ways one could be beautiful—and with this inclusive feed I was curating,

I saw that more bodies looked like mine—I stopped hating my body so much. Stopping the self-hate wasn't the same as engaging in self-love, but it was a great start.

For so many years I had avoided looking in a mirror. I hid behind Barry in pictures because I was ashamed of my body. Can you relate?

Body image is an issue that brings up a lot of emotions and memories, so before we jump into the prompts for this section, I'd like to extend an invitation. At any point along this journey, if the prompts feel more like a personal attack than an opportunity for reflection, I invite you to choose love over fear. Here's a quick example from my own story: When I didn't judge myself in that dressing room in 2016, at the heaviest I'd ever been, I chose love for myself over the fear of being fat. While it has taken years for me to unpack my body image issues, a simple pause to give yourself the space to choose love can be a great place to start.

MINDFUL MILES

Now, you might be thinking, "Sydney, you're asking me to unpack my body image issues by participating in an activity that stirs up insecurities about my body!" And you're right, I am. These questions might make you squirm. I know they did for me when I was first starting out. In fact, I avoided this work entirely until I started hiking. Every attempt I made to sit with my body image issues ended in me not doing the work because I couldn't sit still in a body I felt betrayed by. I invite you to explore this for yourself.

First, try sitting with the following questions and journaling about them. Make note of any thoughts or physical sensations that come up. Next, try going for a walk and reflecting on these questions further. Resist the urge to apply labels like "good" or "bad" to anything you might be feeling. Just pay attention to the difference (if any) between these two exercises. If you try both and still want to run and hide from whatever's surfacing, cultivate curiosity about where these feelings are coming from instead of judging yourself for how you feel.

- If you are fat, have you started to reclaim the word for yourself?

- Is there anything you've been putting off until you reach what you consider to be the perfect weight?

- Where did you learn this idea of what makes the perfect body?

One more thing on the word fat. Yes, the word carries a lot of weight. Yes, it has caused harm for generations. But here's another question: Fat compared to what? To the models that the fashion industry has prioritized because sample sizes require less fabric and therefore generate more profit? Consider who sets the standard of beauty here, and who stands to profit by you judging yourself and others. Reclaiming this word is a radical act that can liberate you from the lies we've internalized as truths about our bodies.

NEXT STEPS

Look in the Mirror

If you've been avoiding mirrors because you don't like what you see, go look in one. Get your face as close to the glass as you can, like I did in the dressing room. Explore the different colors of your eyes, the length of your eyelashes, and how your eyebrows wiggle when you make different faces. Instead of focusing on your body and how it looks, spend at least thirty seconds looking straight into your own eyes. As you do, give yourself compassion, love, and permission to move forward from this point in your life. Whatever happened that brought you to this point is in the past, and no amount of negative self-talk will change it.

Social Media Detox

Go through your social media profiles and look at who you follow. It's time for a detox. As you start scrolling, make note of how you feel when you see certain images. Pay attention to how many bodies you see that look like yours. Does the hot chick on a mountain have you feeling less than? Unfollow or mute. Feeling like you need to buy the latest and greatest from an influencer or brand you follow? Unfollow or mute. If the content someone shares makes you feel bad about yourself or your circumstances, let it go. Anything that doesn't enrich your life, inspire you, or make you feel good has got to go. Shift your use of social media. Is there something you want to learn more about? Follow some accounts that are specific to that topic. Do you want to be inspired by beautiful nature images? Follow some of the photography accounts. Don't torture yourself by staying digitally connected to content that makes you feel bad about yourself. This is your life, your phone, your account, your rules. Your attention is one of the most valuable pieces of currency online today, so don't give another second of thought to the accounts that don't serve your highest good.

Observe Without Judgment

If you're ever feeling consumed by the comparison game, get outside and start observing. If you're in a forest, notice how the tree canopy feels like a nice hug from Mother Nature. Listen to the differences between bird calls. Lie in the grass and look up at the clouds. When we're in nature, we aren't nitpicking the trees, comparing the clouds, or ranking bird calls the way we do human bodies. Allow yourself to simply exist among the beauty of nature and appreciate the diversity you can find.

DEEPER DIVE

It's important to note the difference between consuming information that makes you feel bad about yourself and information that challenges your thinking. When I was first learning about my internalized fatphobia and misogyny, I started following activists and thought leaders in this space. Some of the things they posted challenged my deeply held beliefs about myself, and it didn't feel good. That feeling of being challenged to think differently manifests in my body the same way that feeling bad about myself does. My stomach gets upset, my chest tightens, and I feel a surge of energy as my nervous system gets dysregulated. If we're going to grow and stretch and unlearn the harmful lies we've been telling ourselves, it's going to come with some discomfort. Make sure that in your social media detox, you aren't setting yourself up in an echo chamber. We've lived in these bodies for our entire lives and our beliefs about them won't be unlearned overnight. If you're brand new at this and your feed is a dumpster fire, enjoy some time and space on social media without the posts that trigger your insecurities or fears, and allow this to be a source of inspiration and learning. When you're able to scroll and enjoy it, then you can start to layer in some accounts that will help you learn new things.

CHAPTER 4

RIGHT FOOT, LEFT FOOT

Taking Life One Step at a Time

So now I had the perfect gear for backpacking, but unfortunately the gear couldn't do the walking for me. As we finally rolled up with relief to that mysterious playground in the middle of the Trans-Catalina Trail, I started to execute phase one of my procrastination strategy—bust out the camera to get some footage of me swinging on the swings. My intention was twofold: Delay as much as possible while trying to get the shot, and move as much air across my sweaty body as possible. It was just me and Barry at the playground, nobody else. I took off my pack, enjoying the release as the weight came off of my shoulders.

After ample shots of me on the swings, pointing out plants and animals, and doing everything I could to give my legs a break, Barry started tapping the imaginary watch on his wrist.

"If we want to get to this campground before sunset, we need to get moving. We don't want to be out here in the dark with bison on-trail."

As we packed up, instead of worrying that we wouldn't make it in time, I was inspired by how far we'd already come since we started that morning. I was also thoroughly looking forward to something other than jerky to eat. I wanted a *meal*. Something with substance.

While we were making our way up and down more peaks, I felt my right hip flexor start to get aggravated. I remembered hearing in a yoga class that a lot of trauma and memories are stored in our hips, and for the first time I felt like I understood what that meant. As I was hiking through the pain, I heard a voice in my head. It was my rowing coach from the University of Kansas, forcing me to relive one of the most soul-crushing moments of my life.

"Drive backward with your ass, Sydney."

I was on the erg at the time, an indoor rowing machine, doing sprints with the team after an early morning weight-training session. The mission of the drill was to get our split times as low as possible. No matter how hard I tried, I couldn't get my time down. We focused on my body position, and that's when it clicked for my coach. I wasn't driving with my legs. I was just going through the motions. My form was great, but I wasn't adding power.

I pushed off the balls of my feet, driving back with my butt as I extended my legs, and I felt a pang of pain. I slowed down to a stop and signaled for my coach. Something wasn't right. I made my way down to the athletic trainer's office and sat down on the table for an evaluation. The trainer moved my leg in all different directions, keeping the pressure on my hip flexor area as he manipulated my body position.

"You have a severe strain of your hip flexor," he said. "You're going to need to come see me before and after every practice until we get this sorted out."

I spent most of the spring season on the bench because my hip just wouldn't heal properly. For most of my life leading up to my time on the rowing team at KU, I'd been a cheerleader, so I brought my enthusiasm to practice every day and cheered on my teammates. It was heartbreaking to watch them train and compete without me, but what was I supposed to do? I kept a smile on my face, hoping my enthusiasm would buy me some time to recover and show that I could join them again.

When the spring season wrapped and the coaches were making their selections for the varsity team, I was worried, but I was still optimistic that I would be selected, since they'd said I showed so much promise.

Sitting across from my coach, I listened as she broke the news to me.

"Sydney, you have the best attitude of anyone on the team. It has been an absolute pleasure having you around to cheer everyone on while you've been injured. If we could keep you on to boost morale, we certainly would."

I felt my eyes glaze over.

"But even though your hip has made a full recovery, at the end of the day you're too short to row varsity."

I looked around. I was surrounded by women who were either teeny-tiny and had found a spot on the team as a coxswain—the person who sits at the back of the boat, calls commands for the rowers, and steers—or women who were at least five feet nine inches, some towering above me at six feet tall. I was too big to be a coxswain, but I was too short to match the stroke length and power of my taller teammates.

It crushed me. All of my dreams came crashing down. And for the longest time, I blamed myself for being injured. I was so hard on myself. *If only you'd listened, or asked for help outside of practice. Better yet, if you lost twenty pounds, maybe you could be a coxswain.* Never mind that I'd never wanted to be a coxswain. I just wanted to row.

I stopped hiking and tried to stretch out my hip, shouting ahead to Barry to ask how much farther we had to go before we got to the campground.

"It's on the other side of this peak!"

I rolled my eyes and sighed to myself, remembering the first hike we'd done together. I mocked him in a singsong voice. "It's just around the bend!"

The last climb before Black Jack Campground was aggressive, and we kept getting passed by people who'd started behind us, folks I hadn't seen on the trail until they breezed past us on the last climb before the campground.

On that last climb, I repeated a mantra to myself: "Right foot, left foot."

That came in handy when I had to physically grab my pants and drag my right leg up the mountain. My hip was in so much pain, I cried through the steps, begging and pleading with my body to continue to carry me up the mountain. Every four steps, I would hunch over, sobbing and dry heaving. It felt like I was doing stadiums at KU, running up and down the bleachers for conditioning practice at ungodly hours in the morning. My legs were shaking from working so hard.

"Right foot," I instructed my body, holding on to my pants and pulling my right leg up to meet the left.

"Left foot," I continued, steadying myself before taking a step up with my left leg.

"Right foot," I said, feeling the desire to vomit up all the water I'd been chugging.

"Left foot," I pleaded, as I felt tears welling behind my eyes. *Here we go again. Another cycle that feels more like an exorcism than anything I have control over.* I'd never experienced emotion moving through my body like that. I'd never experienced physical pain like that. All the while we were surrounded by incredible beauty. Between the fields of sage as far as the eye could see, the ocean views, and Barry's random bouts of shouting, "Proud of you!" I could almost forget about the pain.

We crested the top of the peak, and I could see an open field with rolling hills, the antenna on top of Black Jack Mountain, and some small structures. My heart rate quickened, but I tried not to get my hopes up.

I shouted, asking Barry, the island, myself, anyone who might have the answer, "Is that it? Are we almost there?"

As we got closer to the campground, I heard laughter and shouting. *Oh, sweet baby unicorns, we're almost there.*

It was literally around the bend. Knowing we were getting close, all of my pain was magnified. I could feel the dirt rubbing between my skin and my socks. There was a teeny-tiny pebble in my left shoe that kept kicking around. My back was killing me. I had sweat dripping into my eyes, stinging every time I blinked, making my vision blurry. All I could think about was how much pain I was in and how hungry I was. I pulled on my bite valve to get a sip of water, and it took considerably more effort than before, since I was almost out. I wanted to walk faster, but my hiking boots had transformed into cinder blocks, and it was taking every last ounce of energy I had to get to our campsite.

We got to the campground, and I was relieved to see that our site was one of the first ones off the trail. As soon as I sat down, I ripped off my shoes to let my feet air out. My legs were still shaking from the last climb and my pinky toes had turned into blisters. Barry handed me a knife so I could drain them. The moment they started to drain, I felt like a whole new woman.

As I hobbled around, trying to keep my feet clean in the soft dirt, we put up our tiny tent, overlapped our sleeping pads to make it all fit, and started to make dinner. My first dehydrated meal was absolutely delicious. Chicken and dumplings, the highest-calorie meal I'd packed. I was exhausted. I couldn't walk another step. I filled up my water and drank it all. I had to pee, but the idea of walking uphill to the bathrooms sounded like my personal hell. I decided I would do it in the morning. By 6:30 p.m. I was lights out, dead to the world, asleep in our tent.

TRAIL OF LIFE

The fact that I had to devise a procrastination strategy instead of simply asking Barry if we could take a break came from a lifetime of self-gaslighting. My father had an explosive temper, and my mother avoided conflict entirely. Emotional regulation, self-soothing, and advocating for my needs was not taught or modeled for me growing up.

I was told at a young age that my tears were manipulative, and I came to understand that if I was crying, I was manipulating. In fact it wasn't until I was on the trail having these experiences that I allowed myself to cry whenever I felt like I needed to. It wasn't a conscious choice I made, but out in the wilderness, in proximity to my supportive partner, was the first place I felt safe to emote in that way. Now I know that crying is one of the most efficient ways for me to move energy and emotions through my body. I have never gotten done with a good cry and wished I hadn't—I *always* feel better.

I grew up in a home where the punishment for everything was being grounded and sent to our rooms to think about what we had done. When we were free to leave the confines of our bedrooms, we knew we better have a story about what had happened and why. The problem is, when we're young, unless healthy emotional processing has been modeled and taught, we are left to our own devices. I don't know about you, but Little Sydney all the way up to Backpacker Sydney didn't have the basic understanding that my needs are valid, my emotions are valid, my tears are a natural process (not manipulative), and though I might make mistakes, *I* wasn't a mistake.

As a result, I have lived a long life of overexplaining and people pleasing. The thing is, with Barry, I know I don't have to do any of that. He can self-regulate, communicate clearly, he knows what he needs when he needs it, and he isn't afraid to ask for help. He is the first man who has been able to model that for me, and even though we had been together for more than six years when we did our first hike on the TCT, I was still living in my habits that I'd developed when I was younger. Even to this day, after more than thirteen years together, I still catch myself hearing him through the filters of my experiences with my father and reacting accordingly. It's exhausting, and thankfully Barry is patient as I navigate this.

You've probably heard of gaslighting by now, but in case you haven't, it's a form of emotional abuse that uses minimization and manipulation to make someone question their reality. When we self-gaslight, we've internalized these behaviors and abuse and begin to use them on ourselves. This is what it has sounded like for me:

"He didn't mean what I thought he meant."

"They didn't believe my story because I'm not worth believing."

"I should be over this by now."

"My trauma wasn't as bad as theirs. I should suck it up."

"Maybe it wasn't that bad."

Are you living in the same patterns?

When the going gets tough . . . it can be tough to keep going! When we find ourselves struggling to stay motivated in the face of physical pain, social anxiety, or any of the other pressures we experience in our daily lives, it can be helpful to slow things down, put one foot in front of the other, and live life one step at a time. The reality is that life, like that section of the TCT, is full of ups and downs, peaks and valleys, false summit after false summit. When we're hiking, we only have so much daylight, so we have to keep moving forward. As we encounter physical or emotional pain on the trail, it's important to listen to our bodies, trust our intuition, and ask for help if we need it.

MINDFUL MILES

There have been a lot of times where I felt like it was impossible to keep going. When you're "in it"—in the middle of the struggle, *living* the experience but not yet *processing* it, *thinking* about the feelings more than *feeling* the feelings—it can be easy to focus on what isn't working. What is possible when we take stock of what we've been through and draw inspiration from our resilience? If you're "in it" right now, remember that you're still here. Which means you've been "in it" before, and you got out of it, so you'll get out of this too. These prompts can help you draw inspiration from how far you've already come in your healing journey.

- When the going gets tough, how do you keep going? What tools do you have at your disposal to help yourself through hard times?

- Are you an overexplainer? Where did you learn this?

- How have you gaslighted yourself in the past? Where did you learn how to do this?

NEXT STEPS

If the hike gets hard, slow everything down and take one step at a time. Move at the speed of your breath and stop punishing yourself for wishing you were having a different experience. This is your reality right now; the trail isn't getting any shorter, and the days aren't getting any longer. Allow it to suck. In fact, call it out. This is one of my favorite on-trail rituals, either by myself or with a group. It's inspired by one of my favorite movies growing up, *How to Lose a Guy in 10 Days.* In the movie, Kate Hudson's character visits Matthew McConaughey's family and they're playing a card game called Bullshit. As they call out what cards they have, if someone thinks they're lying, they call "Bullshit." Here's how to adapt it for the trail:

1. When the hike gets hard or your brain starts making excuses for why it's hard, say what you're feeling out loud. Shout it. Doing this gets it out of your body and sets up the next step in the game. Are you thinking you're too old, fat, inexperienced, uncoordinated, etc.? We don't want to use these negative thought cycles as mantras, so let's soften them up and separate ourselves from them. Instead of saying, "I'm too fat for this" outright, take a note from Brené Brown, author of *Rising Strong.* She changed my life with six little words: "The story I'm telling myself is . . ."

What feels better: "I'm too old for this," or, "The story I'm telling myself is I'm too old for this"?

2. Call bullshit. Whatever story you're telling yourself about why this experience is unfolding the way it is, call bullshit on yourself. If you're in a group, this is where it gets fun. After you shout out your story in step one, the whole group yells, "That's some bullshit!"

3. Reframe it. How much better does it feel to say, "I've got the rest of my life to do stuff like this!" instead of, "I'm too old for this!" It feels good, right? You're really close to your own stories and have been living with them for years, so the reframe itself might feel like bullshit until you internalize it for as long as you've been holding onto the lies. If you're in a group and you aren't able to find a reframe, let the group know. Chances are, they've said the same things to themselves and can relate. They aren't as close to your story as you are, so they can look at it objectively and help you rewrite the narrative.

DEEPER DIVE

On and off the trail, sometimes our only option is to keep putting one foot in front of the other. If we've lived a life of self-sabotage and negative self-talk, it can be a hard cycle to break. One truth I constantly have to remind myself of is this: Sometimes, the awareness is the work. Sometimes we don't have the resources, support, or capacity to make a change in the moment. In those times, our awareness of our struggle can be a catalyst for change. In the hyperconnected world we live in, with near constant notifications and a lot of competition for our energy and attention, it can feel overwhelming to slow down and create space for the answers to come. When I realized that I couldn't do everything all at once and came to understand that healing is a lifelong journey, it felt like a giant exhalation. Simply removing the pressure to resolve all of life's problems overnight can give way to profound healing.

CHAPTER 5

THANKFUL FOR SNAPS

Unpacking Your Strongest Relationships

When I woke up the next morning, my legs were stiff beyond belief. The night prior, I hadn't even able to make it uphill to the bathroom once we'd arrived at Black Jack Campground. And now there we were, getting ready for another day on the trail. The only things that got me out of the tent were the fact that the trail was mostly downhill into Little Harbor and that we would be stopping at the restaurant at the Airport in the Sky, the island's airport, which sat at one of its highest points. We had a day off in Little Harbor the next day, so I knew once I got through that section of the trail, I'd be able to rest my weary bones for a full twenty-four hours before continuing to Two Harbors.

That was my first breakfast on the trail, and I was really excited about it. I picked the breakfast scramble, a dehydrated mix of eggs, sausage, and hash browns. I enjoyed the ritual of making breakfast in the backcountry—heating up the water, adding it to the bag, and waiting for it to do what it does. I was ravenous. I opened the bag and looked inside. It looked like mush, but it smelled delicious. We had made up a small bag of camp seasoning, which was everything we usually put on our food at home: salt, black pepper, white pepper, crushed red pepper, granulated garlic, thyme, rosemary, and some cayenne. Without it, it was still tasty. With it, oh my goddess. You would think I'd never eaten breakfast before. As I took the first bite, my eyes rolled into the back of my head, as if I had just sunk my teeth into my first Double-Double from In-N-Out.

"Babe, good choice on the breakfast selections!" I called over to Barry as he prepared his food. "This is delicious!"

We finished eating, took our time getting dressed, and packed up camp before setting out for Little Harbor.

The climb out of Black Jack Campground was supposed to be mild according to the map, but it felt like my personal hell. My legs were on fire. The blisters appeared to be multiplying. It took everything I had to not whine all the way down into the canyon. I thought walking downhill was supposed to be easy. It sounded like a luxurious time after a long first day of mostly uphill hiking on the trail. Now that I was doing it, with my toes smashing into the front of my shoes with every step, I was unhappy about going downhill too. It was only two miles to the airport from our campground, but it didn't feel that short. I could finally see the airport building looming in the distance. I watched as planes flew in. We made our way past the soapstone quarry, evidence of where the Tongva, some of the first people to live on the island, carved bowls and tools for trade and commerce. Now my legs were barking something fierce like they did on that last climb before Black Jack the evening prior. I stopped at every switchback to try to catch my breath and chug water. *Will I ever find the balance? Will I ever find flat ground? Will I ever be able to breathe normally? Will I ever be able to hike and* not *be in a tremendous amount of pain?* I paused at some shade before the final path up to the airport and cried. About what, I don't really know, but the frustration and the energy had to go somewhere, and it was coming out of my face.

As I trudged through the final switchbacks, under the sign that welcomes you to the airport, and over to the main building, I was already hungry, even though I had just eaten breakfast. Hiker hunger is real, and my body was begging for calories. In our research leading up to this trip, we'd read a lot about the food at the airport restaurant. Time to see if the bison burgers lived up to the hype.

I saw a bunch of backpacks by the door to the Airport in the Sky Restaurant and followed suit, slinging my pack off my shoulders and once again feeling the sweet release of all the tension, compression, and strain. We swung the doors open like we owned the joint, and marched past a stuffed bison head mounted on the wall and up to the counter to order our burgers.

We filled up our water bottles with cold water and found a seat inside near the windows. I wanted to keep an eye on the area where our gear was because I was not about to lose all of that equipment.

When our burgers arrived, I inhaled mine like I hadn't had solid food in over a year. I'd only eaten two meals out of a bag so far on the trip, but that burger was still a gift from heaven. After we finished our meal, we wandered around the gift store and got back on the trail. I slung my pack over my shoulders, secured my waist belt, secured my chest strap, and found myself checking for my parachute deployment handle, as if my backpack were my skydiving rig and I was preparing for a jump. I giggled at the muscle memory.

Walking back toward the trail, I smiled at the thought of the summer I learned how to skydive. It was the same summer I met Barry, and I'll never forget the day. June 11, 2010. It was a Friday, and I drove out to Chicagoland Skydiving Center to do the ground training required before making my first jump in the accelerated free fall (AFF) program. I read that it would take six to eight hours for a typical student.

As I pulled into the gravel lot, my heart started racing.

Prior to that, I'd completed three tandem skydives (where you're attached to your instructor). When I landed after my first jump in 2005, I knew I wanted to be an instructor someday, and I was so jazzed that I came home and shared the revelation with my parents. They scoffed and shut it down immediately with, "No, you're going to finish your degree." Before my second jump in Austin in 2010, my boss at the PR agency urged me to skip it because I was speaking at a conference the day after the jump was scheduled, and it would be a bad look for the agency if I went splat before my presentation. I did it anyway. After that jump, I knew I wanted to learn how to skydive by myself, and now there was nothing and nobody in my way.

For the first time in a long time, I was choosing something for me—not because my parents had suggested it, not because my friends were doing it, but because I really, truly wanted to—and I didn't care if I didn't know anyone there. I felt empowered as I got out of the car, walking toward what I hoped would be a very exciting chapter of my life.

If I only knew what I was getting myself into.

Once I parked, I took a deep breath. I'd been blasting Kelly Clarkson on the drive out to the country to get pumped up, and I let the song finish playing before I got out of the car, not wanting to interrupt the empowerment session. I'm superstitious like that. I took off my seat belt, grabbed the skydiver's logbook they'd given me the weekend prior, and walked to the small aircraft hangar, where I was told to meet a guy called Barry, who would be my instructor. As I stepped over the short fence between the parking lot and the court-yard, I stumbled, feet-knees-face, into the grass of the volleyball court.

Shit. Skydiving is a sport that requires at least some level of body awareness, and I'd just crashed and burned, not even five steps into the experience. *Shit shit shit shit shit.*

I dusted myself off and looked around. *Did anyone see that?* The place was mostly empty. Only a red Jeep Wrangler and a black

Range Rover were in the lot. I saw a guy sitting on a picnic table—tall and lanky, sun-weathered skin, smoking a cigarette.

"Excuse me, do you know where I can find Barry?" I asked.

He motioned to the hangar behind him.

I stepped inside.

Barry was about my height, and I'm five foot four on a good day. I saw a tattoo on his calf and another that wrapped around his ankle. He walked over and introduced himself.

"Hi, I'm Barry," he said, extending his hand. His eyes were kind, his smile friendly, his demeanor confident.

I shook his hand. "Sydney. Nice to meet you."

The rest of the evening was a blur. He showed me the equipment I would be using, pointing out all of the features. We talked about what we would do on the skydive. He took me over to the parked airplane, and we talked about safety around an aircraft. He explained the structure built to represent an airplane door and showed me how to position myself to exit the aircraft safely. We talked about emergency procedures—what happens when your parachute malfunctions and how to handle it. It was a lot of information.

I'm an active listener, and I like to confirm my understanding by nodding and saying, "Uh-huh," or something affirmative to show I'm comprehending the information.

At one point Barry looked at me and asked, "Are you actually listening or just nodding and saying, 'Uh-huh'?"

"Oh, I'm listening," I retorted.

The final portion of the ground training was a written exam. Being the gold-star-earning, good-grade-getting student I was, I answered all of them right except for one. He told me that he'd been teaching skydiving for more than a decade and that was the shortest ground school he'd ever taught. We were done in less than four hours. He also said he'd never had a student do so well on the test. He was impressed, I could tell.

That night I drove back home to my apartment in the city, and something felt different. I figured it was excitement and nerves around doing my first jump with my own parachute versus being attached to an instructor like I had been for my first three jumps. Little did I know, I'd just met the man I would choose to spend the rest of my life with.

As I followed Barry along the trail, I smiled to myself and felt my eyes well up at the memory of that fateful day. There we were, six years later, married for four, and we were a few miles into the second day of our grand adventure together. We passed the sign that pointed us back onto the Trans-Catalina Trail. We'd been hiking for about five, maybe ten minutes when I felt a rumble in my guts. There wasn't enough time to run back to the airport. It was an emergency.

I was going to shit my pants.

I called ahead to Barry, alerting him that we had a bit of a situation. The trail was open, exposed, and there was very little coverage. I looked around and found a place that was out of view from any of the fire access roads where they hosted ecotours of the island. I was squeezing my butt cheeks together and squirming as I took off my backpack. I found a place to squat, fumbled with my pants—thankful for snaps instead of buttons—and got my pants down just in time not to soil myself.

No no no no no, this can't be happening! I thought. *Why am I peeing out of my butt? Why did this have to happen right now? Is this the end of it?*

I hadn't anticipated that variable. I hadn't even had time to dig a hole. Thankfully Barry had picked up some napkins when we were at the airport so he could blow his nose. When I was done, I stood up, waddled away from the poop on the sloping hill, and pulled my pants up.

I did my best to cover the poop by kicking some dirt on top of it and covering it with some rocks. I had a big bag of jerky in my pack and a small bag of it that I was keeping in my hip pocket for easy access, so I emptied the small bag into the big one and tucked my poop napkin into the small bag. I'd basically failed at the leave no trace rule followed by backpackers, but I'd done my best in an emergency.

We kept hiking, and fifteen minutes later, another poop-mergency. Exact same routine. Scramble to find a place out of view from the dirt roads above and below us, scramble to get my pack off, rush to pull my pants down before it's too late.

"What the *fuuuuuuuuck*?" I screamed silently as I was squatting.

Barry and I had both eaten the burger, so why was my body doing this? Why wasn't *he* pooping all over the trail?

I cleaned myself up and made my way back to the trail, where Barry was keeping watch. We continued our descent into Little Harbor, our first of three beach campsites on the trip.

On the way down, we turned onto a so-called trail called Sheep Chute Road. It was eroded, with deep ruts, and it was steep. At one point Barry started hiking backward downhill to protect his knees. I had to pull over to address one of my pinky toe blisters, and in the process of removing my sock, I ripped off the tape from the blister on my heel, taking the skin with it. Now I had several miles on the steep road, sock rubbing on raw skin, feeling like I'd wrapped my ankle with sandpaper. Turns out downhill all day isn't my jam. My knees were killing me, and I found myself wishing I was a sheep. I figured if I had four legs maybe it wouldn't hurt so bad. That visual made me laugh and gave me a second wind.

We finally made it into Little Harbor, and it was everything the videos and pictures showed and then some. Crystal clear blue water, a sailboat bobbing in the waves in the harbor, a rock formation that looked like a whale's tail, another harbor off to the left, and campsites right on the beach. We found our site, complete with a box for our food and gear, a picnic table, and a shade structure. We took care of our gear, and I made my way down to the water, limping as I went. I was worried about what my heel blister would look like.

Barry grabbed the camera as we went down to the water, and before I walked into the ocean, I took off my sock for the camera, revealing my blister. I walked in slowly and stood where the water would wash over my feet, not submerging them. The water was freezing, and I was not ready for it.

I had to coax myself to walk out farther into the surf, but eventually I made my way to calf-deep, then up to my knees. That was as far as I was willing to go; you couldn't pay me to go any deeper. I walked back over toward Barry, grabbed my towel, and waddled back to our campsite, excited about having a whole day in that island paradise to do whatever I wanted. In that case, what I wanted was to do absolutely nothing.

Mission accomplished.

Our day off was the ultimate lazy day, most of which I spent watching life go by. After we made breakfast, I hobbled down to the ocean to soak my feet. When I returned to camp, I set up shop at the picnic table.

Before we'd left for the trip, Barry had rolled his eyes at me packing my tarot cards. He joked about them every time I said my feet hurt, insinuating that if I hadn't brought them along, I wouldn't have blisters. That the difference between total blister town and healthy, happy feet was completely dependent on whether or not one had a tarot deck on their person.

I sat on that picnic table for hours, asking different questions of the universe and myself, pulling tarot cards, journaling about what the cards meant. All the while, we were watching a bison make its way through the campsites and canyon behind us.

Bison? On an island? Yes. Back in the 1920s, a Western movie was filmed on Catalina. The bison they brought over from the mainland

This is Little Harbor. If you're hiking the TCT, do yourself a favor and spend an entire day here.

were never returned to their homes. The production crew just left them on the island. So there are now more than a hundred bison freely roaming the island. I'd never seen one up close before, and I certainly didn't want them to come any closer, but the bison we saw around the island were truly majestic to watch in the wild.

As night fell, we talked about the plan for the next day. We'd heard the forecasts of rain, but having lived in Southern California for more than five years at that point—and being able to count any significant rainstorms in the region on one hand—we weren't holding our breath.

We'd only brought Barry's ultralight tent. The product description said it was big enough for two people, but as my legs started cramping in the middle of our first night, I wondered how they were measuring people for the tent. One adult and one newborn? Sure. Two six-year-olds? Maybe. Two adults? Seemed like a stretch. Barry and I are both five foot four, so heightwise we shouldn't have felt so cramped, but the tent tapered to a point by our feet. I was seventy pounds heavier than I am now, and as I wiggled around trying to get comfortable, I grew a bit breathless. I finally found a position that didn't cause me pain or induce cramping and I drifted back to sleep, the waves from the ocean providing the ultimate white noise machine. This was the life.

TRAIL OF LIFE

I'm of the firm belief that the relationship we have with ourselves is the most important relationship we'll have in these bodies, in this lifetime. I also believe that the phrase "You can't love someone until you love yourself" is bullshit, because if it weren't for my relationship with Barry, I might not have learned how to love myself. Self-love wasn't modeled or taught in my home growing up, and it was through being loved by Barry that I started to warm up to the idea that I was lovable as I am, without conditions. It is in this relationship where I learned to love myself.

Everyone has different needs and preferences when it comes to love and connection. Some folks are down to roll solo, some folks feel more fulfilled when they're in a relationship. Personally, I couldn't imagine a life without Barry by my side. We're partners in everything we do, best friends who can (and do) tell each other anything, and adventure buddies until the day we die. I know in my soul that we've been together for lifetimes before this one, and I'm so grateful to have the chance to meet up on this planet in these bodies and explore time and space together once more.

Due to how hard I had internalized the trope of "You can't love someone until you love yourself," I carried shame about my relationship status when I was single. I learned early and often that my desire to be in a relationship with someone was desperate. But nothing could be further from the truth. Connection is a basic human desire. If you're not currently in a relationship but want to be, please know you are *not* desperate.

For the folks reading who are rolling solo, living their best lives, and not at all interested in sharing their lives with someone else, I see you too. There are so many ways to live a life, and while a long-term romantic relationship might be the right choice for some, it's 100 percent okay if it's not the right choice for you.

MINDFUL MILES

Giving ourselves time and space to unpack our strongest relationships can lead to a deeper understanding of self. From this perspective, we can more easily see what our non-negotiables are, practice gratitude for the way our people show up for us, give ourselves credit for how *we* show up in these relationships, and use what we find to breathe new energy into our other connections. We're all walking our own Trail of Life and meeting different people along the way. Depending on the season of life you're in right now, your mileage may vary. While the prompts below are about romantic connections (or lack thereof), you can use them to unpack all kinds of relationships—friends, family, colleagues, and more!

- If you have a partner, what do you remember about the day you met?

- If you don't have a partner but hope to have one someday, imagine you're in a safe, loving, committed relationship. Write your story. How did you meet?

- What qualities does your partner possess? How do they challenge you to be a better person?

- If you're single and loving it, take this time to affirm your experience and make a list of the things you're grateful for.

NEXT STEPS

Regardless of our romantic preferences, it feels good to be seen, heard, and understood. If you have a partner, take some extra time to connect in a meaningful way this week. Go for a hike, share some of these prompts with them, and share how you're growing through this process. If you don't have a partner, invite a close friend or family member for a hike or give them a quick call and let them know you're thinking of them.

CHAPTER 6

I CAN DO HARD THINGS

Believing in Yourself

Around midnight I heard a loud crash. I woke from a deep sleep, sitting straight up in the tent.

"What was that?!" I shouted.

Barry sat up in a daze. I panicked, and my first assumption was that we were being attacked by bison.

I wiped my eyes and rubbed my face, trying to catch my breath. Once I figured out where I was and what was happening, I realized it was raining. The loud crash was thunder, not a bison coming to wake us up for a midnight cuddle puddle.

I hadn't been in a thunderstorm like that since we lived in Illinois, and I certainly had never experienced rain like that in a tent. That wasn't really part of the plan, and my groggy brain was having a hard time.

"What do we do? Where do we go? Are we safe?" I asked.

"It's just a little rain," Barry said. "Everything is going to be okay."

I had to pee. Great. The last thing I wanted to do was wear my too-tight shoes and slosh through puddles to get to the porta-potty across the campground.

I grabbed Barry's shoes, put them on my feet, and unzipped the tent. "Just a little rain?" I asked nobody in particular.

As I looked outside, I saw water rushing down to our campsite. We had opted to sleep underneath a tree, and I was regretting that decision. A moat was forming around our tent—there were bison prints right outside it that were full of water. It reminded me of that scene in *Jurassic Park* where they're in the Jeep and you can see the water in the cup ripple and vibrate as the T. rex approaches from the forest.

I looked out toward where the porta-potty was. Hopefully nobody else had to go right then. If I'd made my way out of the tent without soaking my shoes to the sole, that would have been a miracle. If I'd had to stand and wait for someone to finish up, I'd have been done for.

I couldn't run because there were too many puddles to navigate. The gravel road that separated us from the toilets was turning into a mud pit. But I didn't have a choice, I had to go. And after the shitstorm on the way down to Little Harbor, I couldn't trust a fart.

I unzipped the tent the rest of the way, wished Barry a nice rest of his life in case I got gored by a bison on the way to the porta-potty, and clumsily crawled over him to get outside.

I half tiptoed, half hopped around the puddles, navigating the distance between tent and toilet like a battlefield. Every military battle scene in every movie I'd ever watched was now coming to life. I had visions of tucking and rolling to avoid a rogue eagle, as if eagles would be swooping down on humans in a thunderstorm. I imagined a bison waiting for me outside of the porta-potty when I was ready to return to the tent, unsure if he were offering a ride or challenging me to a duel. When I finally made it to the bathroom, I clumsily fumbled for a toilet seat cover and held my breath, assuming it would be the most disgusting porta-potty of all time.

Once I sat down and got my wits about me, I realized I was wrong. It was dry inside. Clean. The sound of the rain on the plastic roof was oddly soothing. I wondered if I could just wait out the storm. But Mother Nature had other plans for me, and waiting it out wasn't one of them, because as soon as I had that thought I heard more rain. Louder. Another crash of thunder.

It was getting worse. I had to get back to the tent.

Making my way back to my cozy sleeping bag was less treacherous, but still scary. I slipped and slid all around the muddy bits. I felt my shoes becoming heavier with accumulated mud, causing my calves and shins to cramp up. I danced and hopped and tiptoed back to the tent, and when I arrived I was exhausted. I unzipped the tent, turned around, and sat down in it backward, with my feet hanging out. I didn't want to bring my muddy shoes into the tent, so I took them off and tucked them under the rainfly, hoping they wouldn't get any worse between now and the morning.

I wiggled my way over to Barry and back into my sleeping bag, checking the tent for any leaks. We were fine, for now. As long as I wasn't getting wet, I could handle it. I started to tell Barry about the battlefield between tent and toilet and drifted off to the sound of rain on the tent.

I slept for another few hours. By the time we woke up the rain had stopped, and we emerged from the tent to assess the situation. As we moved around the campground, we sloshed through the mud. I kept my pack on the bench of the picnic table so it wouldn't get soaked in a puddle. As we were gearing up to leave, it started raining again. I started whining and stomping around like a toddler (one of my better qualities), and Barry offered me his rain gear. My biggest fear was getting wet and then getting cold, so I accepted.

After I put on the rain gear, a ranger pulled up to us in his truck. We asked him about the trail conditions, and I was half inclined to ask him for a ride to Two Harbors. He told us that the conditions on the trail were similar to what we were experiencing at camp, but that it was hikeable. The access roads, however, weren't in great shape. He warned us that if we decided to proceed and something happened that required a rescue, it would take some extra time to get someone out to us. Our choice.

We could wait it out, or we could keep going. Or we could get a ride. We decided to keep going.

As we made our way out of the campground, the rain stopped and the clouds broke. I wore my rain gear for approximately twenty minutes before I took it off again. Between the midnight wake-up bathroom run and that morning's costume change, I was frustrated and cranky.

I lifted my head to check out the views. There was a path that looked like it was going straight up. No switchbacks to make the climb easier, just straight elevation gain. The grade of the trail plus the soft, rocky terrain felt unstable at best. I struggled to keep my feet underneath me, each step squishing and twisting at the end of the stride, each more effort than the last.

"Shifting down a gear!" Barry shouted back to me.

I giggled and sighed. *Will this ever get easier?*

I bent over, hands on knees, trying to catch my breath and give my legs a rest.

"Proud of you!" Barry called out.

"Proud of me, too!" I shouted back.

I continued climbing up the ridgeline of the peak, up and over pieces of white quartz peppered with pink-orange streaks. The entire peak was littered with that stone. It was breathtaking. I kept huffing, kept puffing, cresting over false peak after false peak. As my socks grated on open blisters like sandpaper, I started to cry.

I paused to collect my thoughts. We'd hiked almost twenty-two miles across the island at that point. We'd made it through the longest day, made it through a rainstorm, and we were still there. I was still there. I hadn't been sure I could do it, but there I was, doing the damn thing.

"I can do hard things," I whimpered.

It felt like an admission. A confession, even.

I didn't have the answers yet, but before I'd gotten on the trail, I'd moved away from hating my body. Now I was simply indifferent, and after a lifetime of negative self-talk, indifferent was better than hate.

I kept hiking through the pain.

I can do hard things. I chanted that to myself with every step. It felt like a second wind. "I can do hard things" became my mantra up one of the toughest climbs of the trail so far.

The rest of the hike from Little Harbor to Two Harbors was a mix of steep climbs followed by super narrow stretches, slip-sliding through muddy patches, and with some of the most intense pain I had experienced yet on the trail. The combination of soggy socks and the mud that had accumulated on the bottom of my hiking shoes was oppressive. As we made our way along the final descent into Two Harbors, my muddy boots started to pick up loose gravel. It felt like my feet had turned into cinder blocks once again, and my legs were spaghetti.

By the time we arrived in town, we weren't sure where to go. We took a left toward Catalina Harbor and thankfully a kind couple out for a walk noticed our backpacks and asked us if we needed help. They pointed us in the right direction and told us that camper check-in was on the dock.

We limped our way through town, arriving at the Two Harbors dock. I couldn't see a campground. Were we in the right place? I made my way to the little office and asked where the campground was. I pulled out my reservation paperwork and looked around again. The young man on duty showed me a map. The campground was another mile or so uphill.

Nope. Not interested, I thought. After the day we'd had, the idea of walking farther uphill to sleep in a soggy tent wasn't doing it for me. Our plan for the next day was to hike out to Starlight Beach, out near the very edge of the island, then into Parsons Landing, our last campground on the journey. Our final night would be another remote beach campground, facing the mainland. We were looking forward to watching the New Year's fireworks up and down the coast from the comfort of our campsite.

I asked about the trail conditions for the last leg.

"We'll make the call in the morning," the young man said.

That was my first backpacking trip. I didn't know what that meant, and he could tell.

"The trail is in a questionable condition," he continued. "Depending on how much rain we get tonight, it's possible the trail won't be passable tomorrow. We'll make the call in the morning."

Well, my body is in a questionable condition. I thanked him for the information, and I went back out to talk to Barry.

We had a couple of options. We could make our way up to the campsite and hope it didn't rain. Our gear was already soggy from the night before and my legs were completely exhausted from trudging through the mud, so I wasn't jazzed about that option. They also had these little camping cabins and a community kitchen behind the restaurant. Nothing fancy, just two beds with plastic-coated mattresses, a door that locked, and a fridge. With your cabin reservation, you also had access to the showers.

I was honest about how I was feeling and how much pain I was in. I didn't try to sugarcoat it, and I didn't suck it up and ignore what my body was telling me. I was in excruciating pain between my blisters and sore legs, and Barry's knee was still bothering him from the descent into Little Harbor. Even if the trail was magically in pristine condition, I wasn't confident that my body would be able to get me to the next campground. After a quick deliberation, Barry and I called it. We agreed we wouldn't try to complete the hike. We traded in our Parsons Landing reservations for a camping cabin in Two Harbors for two nights. We would celebrate New Year's with the locals and the other hikers attempting to complete the trail. It was a wise choice. Later we would find out that the storm went down in history among the residents of Catalina Island as "the rain event of 2016."

We tossed our stuff into the room, and on our way to the showers we ran into the couple who had pointed us in the right direction. They were our neighbors! After a little small talk, I expressed my dire need for a shower, and we made a beeline for the bathhouse.

After four days on the trail, and in the worst pain of my life, the shower was absolute heaven. That was the longest I had gone without a shower since Adam had died, and by the time the water warmed up and I stepped in, I felt like I was in an Herbal Essences commercial. I took tender care of my feet, making sure they were clean. As I stood under the hot water I reflected on how far we had come. Just a few short days prior I hadn't known if I could do it. I congratulated myself on hiking more than twenty-six miles of the trail. Even though I hadn't finished it, I did know one thing: I loved my body.

I took that time in the shower to thank each part of my body that had made the trek possible. I started with my feet—my poor, blister-covered feet. I thanked them for their service and apologized for thinking that standing at my standing desk was the same as breaking in hiking boots. I thanked my calves—my massive, swollen, tender-to-the-touch calves—for driving me up ridgelines and keeping me steady. I've always loved my legs, and I thanked them profusely. My legs hadn't worked that hard since I was on the rowing team at KU, and I was extra grateful for their ability to hang in there and keep me going. I thanked my shoulders and my arms for their strength in carrying a very heavy backpack across an island. Finally I touched my stomach.

My stomach has been the source of so much anxiety and shame. I noticed already that my pants were a bit looser after being on the trail. I'd had to sausage-squeeze into the biggest pants that store sold for the trip, and by the end of it they fit relatively comfortably. Instead of viewing my stomach as a mess that needed to be fixed—a part of my body that was unworthy of love and touch unless it was flat and muscular like all the athletes, models, and celebrities I admired growing up—I made a shift. I had long referred to my midsection as my gut in a negative way. In the shower, after the journey, after admitting to myself that I could do hard things, I apologized to my stomach. I apologized for demonizing that part of my body. I apologized to myself for how poorly I'd spoken about myself, about my appearance, for placing so much worth on the appearance of one part of my body. I put one hand on my belly, one hand on my heart, and cried hot tears in that hot shower.

"I knew I could trust you," I said, looking down at my stomach.

That thick, powerful, beautiful part of my body—my gut, my intuition, my inner knowing, my center—had kept me safe and alive for my entire life. It was worth celebrating, not criticizing. After I finished my shower, I took another good, long look at myself in the mirror.

"I love my body, and I can do hard things."

I returned to our camping cabin, where Barry was waiting for me. I felt refreshed, renewed, empowered, and proud. I was also a bit disappointed that we wouldn't finish the trail on that trip.

"To the bar!" he shouted.

We made our way down to the Harbor Reef Saloon, the bar attached to the Harbor Reef Restaurant. As we scanned the menu, I saw a drink called Buffalo Milk, the signature drink of the island. After four days on the trail, that drink was everything I didn't know I needed. It was frozen, and it tasted like a mudslide with banana liqueur added. Topped with whipped cream and freshly grated nutmeg, it was a dream. As we sucked down these delicious cocktails, trying our best to avoid a brain freeze, we scanned the rest of the menu.

The place had a bison burger, a regular burger, and the Harbor Reef burger—a blend of bison and Kobe beef. Considering I'd turned the island into my own personal litter box after the bison burger I'd had at the airport, I was hesitant. Not that I could necessarily blame the burger. Who knew where I'd picked up a bug? But I was cautious. As if on cue, a server walked by with a burger, and my eyes followed them across the bar to the other side, where happy hikers were patiently waiting. I might have actually drooled, because the bartender caught me staring.

I decided it was worth the risk. Barry and I both ordered a Harbor Reef burger. My first Buffalo Milk was already down the hatch, so we ordered another round. When the burgers arrived it was game time. I'd been eating food out of a bag for the last four days, and I was ready for something that didn't need to be rehydrated.

That first bite of the burger was like the first moments of that shower—absolute bliss. I was overcome with endorphins, and my eyes rolled all the way back in my head. Was that the best burger I'd ever had, or was it just how food tasted after days on end of dehydrated meals? Probably a little bit of both.

I looked at Barry. He was having the same experience. I paused and took it all in.

We'd done it.

"We're going to have to come back here and do the whole trail," I said. "You know that, right?"

"Oh, for sure," he replied. "As long as we can get these burgers again."

TRAIL OF LIFE

For three decades leading up to that hike, my relationship with my body had been problematic at best, or outright toxic at the lowest points of my life. Due to the fear of being fat that I'd internalized from my mother, all of my energy was tied up in making sure that I was always in pursuit of a smaller body. The reasons for my self-loathing shifted over time, but every effort that I thought I was making to get healthy was really an attempt to shrink my body. For so long I thought the size

Standing on the dock in Two Harbors, blistered and battered by the trail, already planning our return.

of my body impacted my worth, because in society and at home, bigger bodies were bad and smaller bodies were good.

After that hike, even though I couldn't walk right for weeks, I felt strong, confident, and capable. I carried my curiosity from the dressing room before the hike through to the end of the experience, and one thing was abundantly clear—I loved how spending time outside made me feel. I wanted to do more of it, and I didn't want my body to be the thing that held me back from enjoying it. I was proud of how far I'd come, even if I hadn't completed the hike.

The shift from "What does my body look like and how does that impact my worth?" to "What is my body capable of and how can I honor my inner athlete?" was profound and set me on a path of accepting my body, which was a lot better than hating it.

If I could hike (most of the way) across the island, what else was possible for me? And what is possible for you?

MINDFUL MILES

When we have an experience that affirms that, yes, we can do hard things, it's important to make time to reflect on the experience, extract the lessons, and integrate them into our daily lives. Think back to something you accomplished that surprised you. Have you had a moment that helped you remember that you can do hard things? Sometimes all we need is a reframe to remind us of our power.

- Have you ever thought you *couldn't* do something and then set out to prove yourself wrong? How did it feel to accomplish that thing?

- Take the same scenario or think of a big goal you're considering pursuing. Does it feel different to assume you *can* do it, and then set out to prove yourself right? What does that feel like?

NEXT STEPS

In the years that have passed since my first trek on the TCT, I've refined a process that helps me move through hard things, hype myself up, and celebrate the accomplishment on the other side. Ready to try it for yourself? If you've been following along and doing hikes to correspond with each chapter, you've already done the first two steps. Let's build on this practice together.

1. **Call it what it is.** When I'm leading a difficult hike, I encourage our participants to shout it out when it's hard, when it hurts, or when they're confronting a limitation.

2. **Call bullshit.** The reality is, if you're here and you're reading this book, you've survived every hard thing that life has thrown your way. If your brain, which is wired for your survival, doesn't have a lot of experience in the completion

of hard things because you've heeded its warning every time you've set out to do something difficult, it's time to call bullshit.

3. **If this is possible, what else is possible?** If it's possible that the stories you're telling yourself about why the thing is hard are bullshit, what else is possible? Is it possible that you're completely capable? Is it possible that you've always been?

4. **Believe in yourself.** Even if this is a difficult practice for you, even if your confidence is six feet underground, humor me for a moment. What do you have to lose by believing in yourself? What do you have to lose when you *don't* believe in yourself?

5. **Rinse and repeat.** At any step along the way as you're pursuing a hard thing, when you find yourself telling a story about how you can't, start at the top and keep going. Tuck this ritual away for the next time you need it and remove any shame that comes when you need to use it.

CHAPTER 7

BEING WHERE YOU ARE

Unpacking Distractions

A few months after we got home from the first hike on the Trans-Catalina Trail, I went to Paris with my best friend, Kat. She'd attended culinary school at Le Cordon Bleu and hadn't been back since graduation, so she was doing a little Paris reunion trip, and I decided to crash it.

I'd only traveled internationally with my family, and with Barry for our honeymoon, so it was going to be a new experience to travel solo to meet my friend. Paris was as charming as I thought it would be, and I was in heaven with the food. We walked eleven miles around the city on the first day I arrived, and when we got back, jet lag took me down. We planned to go to the Bastille Market in the morning, and we agreed we'd go by Métro, the Paris subway system. All of my international travel prior to that trip was via cruise ship. So even if we were in a country where I didn't speak the language, the crew did, and if we were onshore, chances were we were on a tour with an English-speaking guide. In Paris, on the Métro, we were the only folks speaking English.

As I looked around, I saw a sea of diversity. People of all shapes, sizes, races, and abilities. I had a very narrow expectation of Paris. Runway models smoking cigarettes while drinking espresso or fine wine. High fashion. Fancy perfume. And don't get me wrong, I found all of those things while in Paris, too, but that first day on the Métro was inspiring.

When I wasn't surrounded with English speakers, I found myself alone with my thoughts. I couldn't understand what they were saying. They could have been calling me an ugly American cow and I wouldn't have known. It felt a lot like when I was on the Trans-Catalina Trail just a few months prior. In Paris, without an international data plan, I wasn't scrolling through the news or social media, so I didn't have that perpetual reminder of how the world was melting down. I looked around at the media these Parisians were consuming. Some were reading books, most had headphones in, but there wasn't a single trashy magazine on the train. No judgments being made about the female form, zooming in on a celebrity's body at the beach, nitpicking cellulite and baby bumps.

It also felt like skydiving in the sense that I was fully in the moment. When I jumped out of a plane, for the minute I was in free fall I was in a total state of bliss. I wasn't worrying about client deadlines, I wasn't checking email; I was just me, fully present, and falling toward an oncoming planet at 120 miles per hour.

As Kat and I counted down the stops until it was time to disembark, I found peace. We made our way to Bastille Market and the sights and smells were incredible. We stopped at an oyster counter and I ate oysters that had been harvested earlier that morning, washing them down with crisp white wine. At an olive stand we tried every variety, while the purveyor hit on Kat and told us both how beautiful we were. When he asked where we were from, we told him California, and he started singing "California Girls." We picked up cheeses and meats and fruits and planned to have the most epic feast when we got home.

We returned to the apartment, got in the elevator, and when we stepped off, I noticed a full-length mirror in the entryway. I grabbed Kat, and we posed for a mirror selfie. That became our tradition for the rest of the trip. Every time we walked past the mirror, we'd snap a selfie. Prior to the TCT trip, I had been hiding in photos. If Barry and I were out and wanted to take a photo, I'd sneak behind him, wrap my arms around his shoulders, and nuzzle my head onto his shoulder. I never let my full body be seen. I don't have many pictures in general from these years of my life, but when we were in Paris, it was a whole different ball game.

I felt confident, like I had on the trail. For the next ten days, that cycle would repeat. Get on the Métro, observe the beauty of humanity in all its forms, feel beautiful myself in the absence of societal messaging telling me I'm not, take a full-body selfie, celebrate life with my best friend. I walked around that city like I owned the joint. I did not expect to feel like a goddess in Paris—a city where I'd assumed everyone would be thin, white, and chic—but I did.

When I returned from Paris, I felt refreshed, energized, renewed. The confidence I'd gained on the TCT carried over into that trip, which gave me so much time alone with my positive thoughts to really soak them in. When I got home, I rushed into Barry's arms and told him everything about the trip. He could tell something had shifted, and he was happy to see me happy.

Once the jet lag wore off, Barry suggested we go paddleboarding. Before the TCT trip and before the time I'd spent in Paris, my mind would have immediately jumped to all the reasons why I shouldn't do that. After hearing his suggestion I was excited, not anxious. The benefits of having so much time to explore and listen to my positive thoughts were now seeping into decisions like that one.

We had never been paddleboarding before but had been discussing it for a while before I left for Paris. I was excited about the prospect of getting out on the water. It made me feel like an official Southern California gal, since it's practically required of San Diego residents to own paddleboards. We were finally becoming real locals!

We bought some boards at a warehouse sale, then made our way to the store to get the necessary accessories and safety equipment. We found stuff sacks to keep our personal belongings dry, tried on life jackets, and as we were getting ready to leave, I realized I didn't have a swimsuit that fit. I hadn't been swimsuit shopping in over a decade.

I walked back to the swimsuit section and picked up a one-piece. White with horizontal navy stripes. I grabbed an XL and a large, the last sizes on the rack, and mentally crossed my fingers. I closed the door behind me, locked it, and paused. I looked at myself in the mirror. I hadn't lost any weight since we'd hiked the Trans-Catalina Trail the year prior. I remembered my pledge to honor my inner athlete and was satisfied that we were taking that step. I took off my clothes and tried on the large suit first. Camel toe. No go. Abort mission.

I wiggled out of the large and into the XL. It fit perfectly.

For the first time in my life, swimsuit shopping wasn't traumatic. In fact, it was empowering. As I stood there in that suit with horizontal stripes—breaking all the fashion rules—I smiled. Continuing the self-love fest from that first shower after hiking twenty-six miles, every part of my body that I had previously criticized was now getting love, affection, and appreciation.

Girrrrrrrrl, I said to myself. *Your butt looks delicious in this suit. Your tattoos are gorgeous. You should show those off more. I know you're not planning on having kids, but you are capable of creating life. You're a powerhouse for humanity.*

I waved my hands around my stomach region and snapped my fingers at myself. My gut was right. I could trust it, and it looked *incredible* in that suit.

I stood up on my tippy-toes. Not to suck in and see what my smaller body could look like. The Paris mirror had helped me break that habit. Instead, the maneuver allowed me to check out my calves. They still had quite a bit of definition from the hike and from all the walking I'd done in Paris. I paused and smiled at myself in the mirror, celebrating how impactful these mindset shifts had been. I went from judging my body on every shopping trip for the first three decades of my life, to curiosity in the REI dressing room, to appreciation after the hike, on the streets of Paris, and now in that dressing room.

I emerged from the dressing room proudly clutching that one-piece. The shopping trip was a game changer in its own right, and I started to wonder if the dressing room was actually a magical portal for self-love and acceptance.

We made a beeline for Mission Bay. We unpacked our boards and started inflating them. Doing that by hand was a workout in itself, and I was exhausted before we got on the boards. Once they were fully inflated, we headed down to the water.

They call it stand-up paddleboarding, but let's be honest: I was on my knees at first. There was no way I'd be able to stand up on that thing—not yet. We paddled out toward a little island in a cove, and when we got there, we took a break. Looking around, I felt the calmest I had felt in a very long time. What was going on? I liked it.

I heard the sound of oars locking into place before I saw them. I instantly connected the dots between my calm and the why, as a rowing team from one of the local universities passed us.

Oh, riiiiight. I was on the women's rowing team at the University of Kansas.

I smiled and cheered and reflected on some of my favorite times on the water with the team. My affinity for water was part of the calm, yes, but I knew it was bigger than that.

We kept paddling, and when we stopped at the next resting place it hit me. As true as it was that my eyes were green and my hair was naturally curly, I maintained a deeply held belief that was challenged in that moment. I believed that if I had the *audacity* to go out in public in a swimsuit and didn't cover up my body, people would be so offended by my appearance that they would drop dead. So, considering the absence of floating bodies in Mission Bay, and having witnessed the rowing team doing sprints as they passed us, it all made sense.

The water is my happy place, and I've been robbing myself of this experience for more than a decade. If folks didn't die at the sight of my body in a swimsuit, what other lies have I been feeding myself?

For the rest of the summer, we paddled as often as we could. Early mornings were our favorite; it was a great way to start the day, and the water was like glass before the afternoon winds kicked up. We did sunset paddle sessions, hauling firewood on our boards from the dock, across the bay to Fiesta Island. After sunset, we would light a fire and just relax until it burned out. We did several full moon sessions too. By the light of our headlamps, the stars, and the moon, we navigated around the glassy bay in the dark, the only folks out there enjoying that experience. It was one of the most magical summers of my life.

TRAIL OF LIFE

A lot of the magic that summer came from how the lessons I learned on the trail were carrying over to other areas of my life off-trail. I didn't realize that I was an expert avoider of feeling my feelings until I started hiking. On the trail, I prefer to hike without headphones, and I keep my phone tucked in my pocket or backpack. It makes sense to me that I'd find peace on the trail, because I'm surrounded by nature and beautiful scenery, listening to the birds and watching other animals doing what they do. On the Paris Métro, without an international data plan, without an understanding of the language being spoken around me, I was also able to find peace, just like I had on the trail. Paddleboarding brought me back to the water, where I've always felt powerful and strong, and put me right in the path of a collegiate rowing team. While these experiences are all very different, the common theme is a disconnection from distractions.

When we give ourselves a chance to disconnect, we can hear our inner voice. And I don't know about you, but I had been ignoring mine for most of my life. I'd watch TV, listen to music, overcommit at work, prioritize someone else's needs above my own, do nearly *anything* to avoid being alone, still, and quiet.

The act of disconnecting is almost radical in today's day and age. We carry miniature computers in our pockets and have access to more information than ever before. While capitalism has opened the door for brilliant innovations and technological advances, it has also shifted our society's expectations that things happen overnight and at lightning speed. This is also overloading our systems—mentally, physically, spiritually.

MINDFUL MILES

There are so many things competing for our attention—our own lives, the needs of our community, and what's happening around the world with our fellow humans. We have access to so much information, it's no wonder we're overwhelmed, burned out, and feeling like there isn't enough time in the day to do whatever we need to do, let alone what we *want* to do. Use the prompts below to do a quick check-in with yourself.

- When was the last time you sat in silence without distractions? When was the last time you spent more than two days away from your phone?

- If you've never spent time away from your phone, social media, emails, etc., is it possible that you're trying to distract yourself from something? (Note that the first thing that comes to mind when we answer that question is usually true.)

- When was the last time you asked your body what it needs? Have you ever given it a chance to answer?

NEXT STEPS

After unpacking your distractions, you might become painfully aware of how tethered you are to technology, the needs of others, and the alluring promise that productivity equals success. Here are a couple of suggestions to help you tap into mindfulness and act on your new awareness.

- Do you commute to work? How long does it take? Do you commute in silence, or do you usually listen to music, a podcast, scroll through social media? Try going without music. Without a podcast. Without scrolling. Pay attention to what thoughts come up. Pay attention to your surroundings. If you're on public transportation, what's the energy like? If you're driving, pay attention to the other drivers and notice what sensations you experience during the commute. Allow your thoughts to be like passing clouds versus something you have to lasso and trap.

- Different phones have different settings for monitoring screen time. Find yours, look at where you're spending your time, and ask yourself: What else could I be doing with this time? I was shocked to see how much time I spend on social media (outside of my work duties and research). When I dialed back my personal connectivity, I gave myself that time back and used it to my advantage instead of leaking my attention like a sad balloon to activities and people who weren't going to help me get closer to my goals.

CHAPTER 8

LET THE DIAGNOSIS SET YOU FREE

Releasing What No Longer Serves You

I woke up on September 18, 2017, in excruciating pain. It felt like someone had taken a corset, shoved it into my midsection through my belly button, wrapped it around my intestines, cinching it down, tightening around all my internal organs. It was awful. My first thought was appendicitis, and I got scared. I told Barry what was happening, and we rushed over to urgent care.

Once I checked in and was called back to the exam room, everything was a blur. The folks at the hospital didn't seem to be interested in the story as to what led to these symptoms; they were just interested in the symptoms themselves. The first nurse I spoke to said I probably had Crohn's disease.

What the hell? Adam, my friend who died on the BASE jump, had lived with Crohn's disease, and I knew from his lived experience, his descriptions of what his life was like while managing that disease, that what I was experiencing was *not* what he had. I was flabbergasted that a nurse would jump to a chronic diagnosis. After they did a full blood draw, they sent me home with supplies to collect stool samples to rule out any viruses or parasites. For three days I pooped into a plastic container I put over the toilet, scooped out a little bit, and put it in a vial with some kind of solution. I returned the samples to the lab after my third poop and scoop. Later that day, as Barry and I were pulling into the arrivals section at San Diego International Airport to pick up a friend I hadn't seen in a while, I received a call from the hospital.

This isn't the best place to receive test results, I thought. I answered the phone reluctantly.

"Hi, Mrs. Williams?"

"Speaking."

The person on the other end introduced themself as a nurse from my doctor's office. My test results were in.

"You have type 2 diabetes," she said.

I felt tears sting my eyes. My heart rate quickened. I thanked them for the information and hung up.

My mind was racing. I didn't know what the disease was. I didn't know what was happening inside of my body. All I knew about diabetes was the stigma—that poor, lazy, morbidly obese, and old people get it. I had heard that advanced stages of diabetes could lead to foot amputation. But I didn't know why it was happening to me. Was it hereditary? Could I cure it? Would I be living with it for the rest of my life? How did we get there?

Well, I guess I can't eat bread anymore.

I was crying at that point, trying to hold it together, not wreck the car, and safely pick up our friend. Barry looked at me and told me we'd figure it out. That everything would be okay. I wanted to believe him. I wiped my face as we pulled up to the curb. Pleasantries were exchanged, and not surprisingly, my friend was starving after the flight from Chicago.

We made our way toward the beach to our favorite sandwich shop. As I read the menu options, I was overwhelmed. What did that food do to my body? Did it make my blood sugar better or worse? What can I eat? I figured I was already diabetic, and one more sandwich wasn't going to make or break it, so I got my usual—a turkey club, bacon extra crispy, with avocado. We grabbed the sandwiches and walked across the street to enjoy them on the beach. We found a bench on the cliffs near the Pacific Beach Pier, and I held up my sandwich to the sky, toasting to what I imagined would be my last meal that included bread.

In my mind, I had a little dialogue with my last sandwich, shedding a single tear as I held it up.

Hey, bread. It's Sydney. I think we need to break up. It's not you, it's me. Thank you for all of the energy, nourishment, and comfort you've provided over the years. I just got diagnosed with type 2 diabetes, so I'm pretty sure we can't hang out anymore. Thank you for being such a pleasurable part of my life, but I'm afraid we have to part ways now. See ya later, carbs!

The adjustment into managing diabetes was excruciating. On our anniversary, Barry and I went to Juniper and Ivy, one of our favorite restaurants in San Diego. Richard Blais from *Top Chef* opened the restaurant as one of his experimental kitchens, and it is one of our go-to places to take out-of-town guests or celebrate special occasions.

Sitting at a corner table, looking at the menu, I started to cry. I was in the process of figuring out which foods were contributing to my elevated blood sugar and which ones were helping keep it stable, and I was overcome with deep sadness.

Throughout my entire life, food has been an expression of love. My father grew up around the restaurant industry and worked in hospitality during his twenties and into his thirties. He taught me how to cook, and some of my favorite childhood memories were made in the kitchen. I took to cooking quickly, and when I worked in restaurants to put myself through college, I developed a palate for fine dining and great wine. As I got older and life started getting harder, cooking was my escape. When the world was just too much, I'd find myself picking an elaborate recipe that I could get lost in.

Barry also loved cooking. He loved any excuse to get creative with food and beverages, or even create a whole menu around a specific theme. Spending time in the kitchen together was how we celebrated and shared our love for each other.

In my most important relationships, food was the centerpiece. A safe space. A creative outlet. What was diabetes going to do to that part of my life?

I looked up from my menu at Barry, who had reached out for my hand. I was afraid to take it because if I had the slightest bit of human touch, I'd turn into a puddle. My defenses would be completely down, and I would have no energy left to retain the tears welling up in my eyes.

I grabbed his hand and let the tears fall. "Is this what the rest of my life is going to be like? Crying over menus? Unable to celebrate with food anymore?"

He squeezed my hand and assured me again that everything was going to be okay.

Thankfully, the hospital had a great diabetes education program. Honestly, I hope every hospital does, because diabetes is an epidemic. In my classes at the hospital, I learned a terrifying statistic: More than half of the adults in the United States are prediabetic or living with diabetes, according to the American Diabetes Association.

My doctor gave me a range of where my blood sugar readings should be when I wake up, after eating, and before bed. The analyst part of my brain needed data, so I would eat something, wait a bit, then check my blood sugar. Rinse and repeat. I did that until I identified foods that were delicious and kept my sugar levels in the safe zone. I also learned that there are four factors that affect your blood sugar: food, exercise, medications, and stress.

I'm a gold-star-earning student, and I was determined that I would be the best damn diabetes patient that hospital had ever seen, so I took to the first three factors right away, doctor's orders. The fourth . . . well, we'll get to that.

First up: food. I took a good, hard look at the food I was eating and cleaned out our house. Everything that I knew would elevate my blood sugar got tossed. We stocked the fridge and pantry with things I knew I could eat. I had been eating like a twelve-year-old boy leading up to my diagnosis, so Barry took one for the team and finished the frozen pizzas and Ben & Jerry's, while I replaced them with more vegetables. Leading up to my diagnosis, it was normal for me to drink a bottle of wine by myself every night, if not more. After my diagnosis I stopped drinking—if I wanted to manage the disease effectively and aggressively, drinking my calories was a surefire way to sabotage the mission, so I quit altogether.

Second: exercise. There was a canyon leading up to our street, and I started walking it every morning. It took about forty-five minutes to get from our front door, out to the canyon, down one side, up the other, and then turn around and come home. We purchased some TRX straps and turned the tree in the backyard into a bodyweight gym. I picked a few exercises from the poster that came with the straps and created a workout routine to do when I got done with my morning walk.

Third: medications. I started taking metformin as prescribed. Prior to my diagnosis I wasn't on any medications. After my diagnosis, I was taking metformin twice daily, and the doctor wanted to add a prescription to correct my cholesterol levels as well. I wanted to try to correct the cholesterol naturally through diet and exercise, since I'd already made major lifestyle changes following my diagnosis. I remember feeling scared to advocate for myself, to suggest the diet and exercise route before adding another medication to my routine. We have a choice when the doctor tells us what to do. I'm glad I spoke up, and I'm glad she agreed.

Those quadrants—the four factors that affect your blood sugar—became my whole life. When I woke up in the morning, if my blood sugar levels were higher than the range specified by my doctor, I would scan the four areas. *What did I eat yesterday? Did I move my body? Did I take my medications as prescribed? How's my stress?* Throughout the process of learning how to live my life with diabetes, it became abundantly clear to me how difficult the disease would be to manage at other stages of my life. I felt fortunate to have the time and resources to manage it as effectively as I had been, because for so many Americans and people with diabetes around the world, that isn't the case.

My physical body started seeing results, as one can expect after making dramatic lifestyle changes. Between my diagnosis date and mid-November, I had lost around fifteen pounds. However, my blood sugar levels were still elevated. I had my nutrition dialed in, I was walking every morning, and I was taking my medications at the same time every single day. That last quadrant, stress, was what I needed to address. So I dug deeper and did a scan of the different elements of my life.

Friends? Super solid, feeling very supported.

Marriage? My husband is a saint and is making these lifestyle changes right by my side; he's all in on helping me manage my diabetes.

Work? Ding ding ding.

At the time I was diagnosed, I was back at the marketing firm I had worked with before I left corporate America to skydive full-time. In my role as director at the firm, I was leading email marketing efforts for NBC, and my diagnosis came the week before fall premieres—easily one of the most stressful times of my career.

I knew I needed to make some changes in my professional life if I wanted to manage the disease effectively. While I had everything else dialed in, the one thing that remained was the stress. I had to get to the root of it.

I worked remotely from our house in San Diego, but I was staffed out of the San Francisco office. It was common for me to fly to SF in the morning and fly home that evening. Every week I took the train up to

LA and spent at least two days in the NBC offices, if not more. The travel was stressing me out, so I made the case to stop doing it. I prioritized doctor's appointments instead of working them in around my career. Reducing my travel schedule helped with the stress, but it wasn't enough.

When you work in an agency setting, you're on client time. If they need you, they need you. For over a decade I had been prioritizing client needs over my own. Something had to give.

On the side, I was helping my friend Brenda with the branding and marketing for her startup. I knew joining a startup wasn't going to reduce my stress, but I figured if the work I was doing was something I cared about—in that case, an all-natural skin-care line that called out unrealistic standards of beauty and the oppressive systems that created them, while prioritizing women's empowerment and social justice—perhaps I could reduce my stress after all. I started toying with the idea of leaving the agency to join her team, and suggested to my friend that, when she was ready to make her first hire, I was interested in talking about what that could look like. I didn't know if that was actually on her radar, but you never know until you ask.

There were a lot of factors to consider in that kind of a decision as well. I knew my friend couldn't pay me what I was earning at the agency. I knew she couldn't offer benefits that would compete with unlimited vacation time and platinum-level health care.

There are a handful of people I turned to when I was making big life decisions like that. Barry, of course, as those decisions directly affected him and our quality of life. My mentor, Aaron, who had been helping me navigate my career and life since we met at the SXSW Interactive conference in 2009. My best friend, Kat, who knows me better than I know myself most of the time. And of course my family.

Fortunately, all these big changes were happening around the holidays, and I hadn't seen my family in years. Flying my entire family from Orlando to San Diego felt like a very adult thing to do. That way

I could check a bunch of boxes—do something nice for my father, whose birthday periodically falls on Thanksgiving, see my sister and her boyfriend, and show off the life Barry and I had created for ourselves on the other side of the country. Given all the changes that were happening in my life as it related to managing my diabetes, I also wanted to get their opinion on the startup.

The week my folks were in town was magical, and my whole family fell in love with San Diego. What's not to love about living in a place that is seventy-two degrees and sunny most of the year? We talked about the option of me working for the startup, and my parents were enamored by the prospect of me becoming a millionaire and buying property on Sunset Cliffs Boulevard with a casita in the back for them to call home. Memories were made, life was good. To add to the joy, by the end of the trip my sister and her boyfriend decided they wanted to get married. On New Year's Eve.

In prior chapters of my life, when I was trying all the diets and fad workouts, I would consistently get offtrack with whatever plan I was on during the holidays and beat myself up about it endlessly. That year was different. The first fifteen pounds I lost before the holidays could be attributed to the lifestyle changes I had made immediately following my diagnosis. After my family returned home from their visit, I had a hard time getting motivated to get outside for my daily walks. The food I ate was changing, as it tends to do during the holiday season. I was still taking my medications as prescribed, and though my blood sugar levels were trending down, the numbers on my glucometer were still higher than the target ranges my doctor had given me. Much like that trip to the Encinitas REI store, I wasn't judging myself about failing to stay on track. I was curious about how it was possible that I could continue to see progress despite getting offtrack with my diabetes management plan. It wasn't until I got home from my sister's wedding and lost another ten pounds that I started to connect the dots.

When Barry and I flew to Orlando for my sister's wedding, we stayed with my parents. When we got to their apartment, Barry and I snuggled up in the big leather chair in their living room and clarity hit me like a ton of bricks. Growing up, my sister and I argued a lot, and sometimes the insults cut deep, lodging themselves into my brain and informing my beliefs about myself. For most of my life, I'd been carrying the weight of all the horrible things my sister had said to me over the years. That I was a bad person. That I was a bitch. That I was stupid. And for just as long I'd been trying to prove her wrong. As we got older, the comments slowed down because we weren't bickering children anymore, but every once in a while, she'd launch a zinger that would bring me right back to our childhood spats. Truthfully, it was near impossible for me to hear what she was saying without the filters of my pain. There had been enough conversations that ended with me and my hurt feelings that I was bracing for insults, even if that wasn't her intention.

Sitting in that chair, being swallowed by worn brown leather and wrapped up in Barry's arms, I sobbed. When I was thinking about the weight loss between Thanksgiving and my sister's wedding, I couldn't wrap my head around how I was still losing weight despite the changes to my diabetes management routine over the holidays. Sitting in that chair, having released a lot of emotional weight as I processed these truths, it was clear to me—when I healed emotional wounds, my physical form would follow. Bringing my family to my house for Thanksgiving made me feel seen, heard, understood, and inspired for the first time in years. The weight I was carrying was not limited to the pounds of flesh and bones on my physical frame; it lived in my tissues, in my spirit, and in my mind.

TRAIL OF LIFE

Looking back, receiving that diabetes diagnosis set me free. It gave me permission to take my life into my own hands and make the changes

I knew I should have been making from a place of love for myself over the fear of the stigma of the disease. When I was making decisions in the spirit of managing diabetes, everything felt more empowering than when I had attempted to prioritize my health in previous chapters of my life. The diagnosis and the four quadrants my doctor gave me led to a new framework through which I came face-to-face with some of the contributing factors that led to the diagnosis. As a result, my affirmation during the following months became, "I release what no longer serves me."

I first heard this phrase when I was taking a course and the facilitator was talking about negative thoughts. She simply said, "Did you know you can just release your negative thoughts? It's like you have a balloon in your hand, and the balloon is the negative thought. All you gotta do is let go of the string!"

I thought she was batshit crazy. You can just let it go? And that's it? The negative thoughts never come back? It felt so shallow, so woo-woo, so . . . surface. There was no acknowledgment of different barriers a person might face. Like trauma. Being in my body didn't feel safe back then, and my negative thoughts felt like a warm blanket, protecting me from the vulnerability of being optimistic. If I were already angry and sad, then nobody could hurt me further.

Once I was diagnosed with diabetes, it was like a red flag from my body.

"Hey, down here! We've been trying to get your attention! Did it work?"

As I started to manage the disease, I had no choice but to be in my body, curious about what was happening in it. Almost immediately, "I release what no longer serves me" came to mind. I had a lot of unlearning to do.

A lot of the habits I had developed over the course of my lifetime—in a state of unresolved and unacknowledged trauma—had gotten me into this position, so I turned to this trusty phrase. I had nothing to lose (except the negative thoughts) and everything to gain. So I gave myself permission to release the behaviors, beliefs, and relationships that were no longer serving me. Anything that could possibly be contributing to this disease had to go.

When I was eating what I thought would be my last sandwich in the hours following the diagnosis, I had no idea that I would soon come to realize that diabetes was the best thing that had ever happened to me. These days, I'm the happiest and healthiest I've ever been. My diabetes is in remission, and I've built a life that will help me continue to manage this disease via nourishing foods and mindful movement.

Can you say the same for yourself? Is there something you've experienced on your Trail of Life that has transformed your life for the better?

MINDFUL MILES

At some points in our lives, we will be crystal clear about what we want and why we want it. We will move mountains to achieve our goals. Other times, we may need to throw up our hands and say, "I don't know what's next, but this ain't it." In these moments, we must make an active choice to move forward regardless. While this can feel frustrating, knowing what you *don't* want—or knowing what you're ready to release—can shift your energy and provide you with a new perspective.

- As you were reading this part of my story, did anything come up for you? What are some of the things that you've been carrying that you'd like to release?

- Where were you the last time you got shocking news? What do you remember from that day? What has happened since then?

- If you're living with prediabetes or type 2 diabetes, or another chronic condition, what actions are you taking every day to manage the situation?

- If you're currently trying to manage your physical weight, are the actions you're taking for your physical health supportive of your emotional, mental, and spiritual well-being?

NEXT STEPS

Even before I started hiking and had this awareness of how nature was helping me come back to myself and find healing, I gravitated toward wide open spaces. It started on our family vacations. My father is a travel writer and photojournalist specializing in cruise vacations. To date, I've been on more than twenty cruises to various points around the world, and on our days at sea between destinations, I used to love sitting on a deck chair and getting lost in the ocean views. I loved being surrounded by water on all sides, without another ship, landmass, or sign of humanity in sight. Though days at sea were usually very windy, I loved how the calming blue tones of the sky and the sea balanced out the chaos and noise of the wind on deck.

Since those early days of finding peace on the deck of a cruise ship to present-day, wide-open spaces have given me an opportunity to settle into my thoughts and tap into a sense of possibilities. Whether it was going for long drives on country roads in the Midwest, counting shooting stars while looking up at the night sky, staring out at a desert landscape, or getting lost in my thoughts as I gazed upon a mountain range, my worries tended to melt away. Maybe it's the vastness that puts my existence and my problems into context, or perhaps it's as simple as being still long enough to settle in with my thoughts. Once we moved to San Diego, whenever I needed to clear my head, I would go to Sunset Cliffs. There's something extra magical about sitting on the edge of a continent with nothing between you and the horizon—ocean as far as the eye can see.

In my outdoor adventures, I've spent a lot of time on windy ridgelines and summits, and over the years, I've developed a practice that helps me get back into my body, connect with the world around me, and find a bit of peace. Here's how I use the wind to my advantage:

- Find a windy spot. This could be at home, on the street, out in nature.

- Think of the things that have been weighing you down recently and scan the different areas of your life—your health, social circles, relationships, family, school, work, parenting, etc.

- Once you have a list of the things that are weighing you down, imagine how much lighter you would feel if you were able to let them go. Visualize the weight coming off of your shoulders, your mind clearing, and your body feeling calm and peaceful.

- Face into the wind with your arms outstretched. Visualize the wind carrying your worries away. Whatever is stacked up on your shoulders is scattering into the wind and freeing you from the weight.

- Do this for as long as you need to. If you get distracted or your arms get tired, take a break and turn around.

- With your back to the wind, think of all the things you're striving for. Whether that's a promotion at work, a healthier lifestyle, a new connection—call it in. Ask for what you want.

- When you have a list of things you're striving for, feel the wind on your back. Whatever you're up against, no matter the level of support you have—the wind, the universe, God, unicorns . . .

whatever you believe in—it has your back. What is meant for you will always find you. Breathe in the support, exhale your self-doubt.

- Rinse and repeat as often as necessary.

This, like any ritual, is not a one-and-done kind of thing. When we think about our trauma packs, we can't see all of the contents at once unless we unpack the whole thing. So if you get through your top-of-mind list, feel the release, and then other things that weren't in your current awareness come forward, don't get discouraged. Healing is a lifelong practice. When you let these thoughts and experiences go and something comes zooming in behind them, you might feel discouraged, but think about this: If you never released the first round of thoughts, you wouldn't have the awareness of what else needs to be healed. This is great news! It's working! You can do it!

CHAPTER 9

ON THE COUCH, WATCHING "THE BACHELOR"

Unpacking Your Stories

After my sister's wedding, I jumped right back into work. The first two weeks of January felt like two years. Every day dragged on forever. I was in back-to-back meetings for eight hours a day and barely had time to get my work done between calls, let alone eat, drink water, and take care of myself. I started having panic attacks. I couldn't peel myself away long enough to rest and recover. Not only was I managing NBC's email marketing, but I was also the lead on a national commercial campaign. My stress was through the roof. There was one saving grace, however. A little pocket of inspiration.

Between Thanksgiving and my sister's wedding, on my weekly train ride up to LA to work in the NBC offices, I had shared a photo on Instagram outlining my experience managing diabetes so far. It was the first time I'd posted about the disease publicly, so I had a lot of anxiety around that post, but I decided to tell my anxious brain to take a back seat and let the words flow from my heart. Looking back, I'm glad I found the courage to share the way I did, because within days of posting that photo, I got a note from a director and producer from a medical media company. They wanted to follow me and Barry around for a few days and shoot a multimedia documentary about my life since being diagnosed with diabetes. What the heck? When I saw that message come through, I thought surely it must be some sort of scam. That kind of thing only happens in the movies. *I make one post and now this?* I decided to get on the phone with the team to further evaluate the opportunity, and I'm glad I did.

I also realized that for my entire career I had been teaching people how to numb themselves. When I was managing email marketing for NBC, I wanted you to sit on the couch and binge-watch TV shows. When I was launching a new wine brand, I wanted you to drink lots of wine. When I was writing hilarious hot dog puns as the Wienermobile on Twitter, I wanted you to eat lots and lots of hot dogs. And when I taught David Arquette how to tweet from a plexiglass box on top of Madison Square Garden, I was slinging Snickers candy bars. Everything I thought was a bragging point on my résumé wasn't worth bragging about after all. I was a by-product of the work I had been doing—sick, numb, tired.

Fortunately, my friend Brenda had run the numbers on her startup and said she was in a position to make her first hire. Between the agency being so stressful and watching my daily blood sugar readings continue to rise, I knew something had to change. I accepted Brenda's offer to join the startup as chief marketing officer, and I would start in February.

The diabetes documentary shoot was scheduled for January 19. I wanted it to be the beginning of the rest of my life. New job, new outlook, a clean slate.

On the day I called the agency to tell them I was resigning, I felt like I had lost another hundred pounds. I felt free. The commercial campaign no longer felt like life or death, because I had chosen life.

Later that evening, Barry and I had dinner with the production crew for the documentary. As we sat down at our booth at Juniper and Ivy with the director, producer, and photographer, I shared the story of how just a few months prior, I was crying over the menu at the same restaurant, unsure of what the future would hold for me. In some classic get-to-know-you questions, the photographer asked me what I do for work. I shared that I had quit my job earlier that day to pursue a new role. The words *chief marketing officer* rolled off my tongue, and I felt so satisfied with myself. I had set an internal goal to be CMO by the time I was thirty-five, and here I had just accepted a role with that title at thirty-two. I savored that self-congratulatory feeling for all it was worth. After so many years of trauma and pain, it felt good to feel good again.

As dinner carried on, I could feel that we were in for a treat for the shoot. These folks were not sleazy production types looking to sling products that nobody needs. They were storytellers. Dot connectors. I knew I was in very good hands.

On the morning of the first day of the shoot, I was showering, listening to my usual playlist, when a song came on that I didn't recognize. In fact, for the first two-thirds of the song it didn't even register with me. One lyric jumped out, and it was a voice I recognized: Kyle from Slightly Stoopid, a local reggae band. I was a Slightly Stoopid superfan, and I was amazed that I hadn't heard that song before.

The song was "Choice Is Yours" by a band called Stick Figure, and the lyric that caught my attention was about how, in every situation, everyone has a choice, and we can't please everyone all of the time.

After hearing those words in the shower, it clicked for me. I had been living a life trying to please everyone—my family, my colleagues, my husband, my friends—and it wasn't until the day before hearing that song that I had chosen me. Sure, I had bouts of choosing things for myself here and there, but overwhelmingly I was living my life for someone else.

I had checked all the boxes. I went to college, I got my degree, I had a good job, I was making lots of money. But I wasn't happy, and

I certainly wasn't healthy. It also hit me like a ton of bricks that it had been my choices—good, bad, or indifferent—that had gotten me to where I was. Literally in the shower in our gorgeous bungalow in San Diego, thirty-two years old, having just quit a super-cushy corporate marketing job to join my friend's startup as a newly diagnosed diabetic.

The choice was mine. Diabetes empowered me to see that and truly understand it. As I became aware of the fact that I had a choice in everything I do—and as I made different choices—my life started to improve dramatically.

The goal for the first day of the shoot was to get the interview portion done. As the trucks full of production equipment pulled up, we ushered the lighting and sound guys, along with all their equipment, into the house. Our home had just turned into the set for the documentary. While they were setting up the room for my interview, the photographer and I went down the street to get some stills while the morning light was still soft.

I had never done a photo shoot before, and it was brutally apparent. I was so awkward. Any expectations I had for a photo shoot were rooted in what I saw on TV or in movies. Of course, I had been part of shoots over the course of my career for commercial projects, but it was quite different being on the other side of the camera. I didn't know what to do with my face. I didn't know where to look. I didn't know what to do with my body or how to pose. Tom, my photographer, was kind, patient, and, fortunately, insanely talented at his craft, because at each location it would only take a few clicks of the camera to get what he wanted. I had envisioned fans blowing my hair like Beyoncé, cameras clicking hundreds of times to get the shot, being told to channel my inner lion or tiger, and to flash my best Blue Steel. None of that happened. I just walked around the neighborhood, and when Tom saw the shot he took it. Easy peasy.

Over the course of the rest of the shoot, I felt so alive. After we wrapped on the interview, we collected B-roll. Shots of me sitting on the rocks looking pensive, of Barry and me riding bikes around Coronado Island, paddleboarding at sunrise, cooking at home . . . and all of it was magical. The most impactful part of the whole journey, however, was seeing Barry's interview portion. It was so powerful to hear Barry speak about what it was like to witness me managing the disease, taking the mountain that is diabetes and breaking it into baby steps. To hear him tell the camera how much he loved me, how much he believed in me, and how he couldn't wait to see where I went from there, was further confirmation that our connection was as strong as I knew it to be. And in the midst of hearing these words, I was reminded of the last time I felt so validated, so seen, so supported.

Prior to my diabetes diagnosis, I shared something with Barry that I hadn't shared with anyone else. We were on the couch, watching *The Bachelor.* Judge me if you want, but I've learned a lot about what *not* to do in relationships by watching that show.

On the episode we were watching, the women were huddled up on a couch in the mansion. One of the contestants said something about an incident that had happened to them and that they never really talk about it with anyone because they're afraid of what people will think of them. Barry paused the show and turned to me.

"Do you worry about that?"

"Worry about what?"

"Do you not talk about things that happened to you because you're afraid of what people will think?" he asked.

"Oh yeah, lots of stuff," I replied.

Like how I was raped twelve years ago.

"I just can't believe how women are conditioned to not talk about things that happened to them," Barry said. "Things that are out of their control. I could never judge a woman for something that happened to her."

I realized in that moment I hadn't felt safe enough to share that story with anyone. I was in my twenties when it happened, and on my couch some eleven years later, I truly felt the weight of the secret I had been carrying by myself for all that time.

At that point I had been with Barry for seven years, and I hadn't told him anything about it. Not because I didn't trust him, but because I had buried that part of my life for so long. I swore I would take it to the grave. When we met, I had been having wonderful, healthy sex and figured if the act of sex itself didn't trigger me, then I had definitely worked through all the trauma from the rape. And God knows I didn't want to scare that man away with my baggage.

I didn't say anything that night, but my wheels were turning.

Why didn't I tell anyone?

I had a flashback to when I was a kid. I was in my childhood bedroom, playing with my Beanie Babies. I had quite the collection and had recently built a village for my Beanie Babies out of old boxes, the latest iteration including an elevator made out of an old Jones Soda six-pack container.

Next I decided to fashion a feeding trough out of a soap box, using a box cutter to remove a panel from the box, leaving a wide, shallow trough where the animals in Beanie Baby Village could all congregate and feed.

As I was cutting the final side, the knife slipped and sliced my palm open, about an inch long and deep enough to draw blood, but not require stitches. While I was trying to keep my hand from bleeding profusely, I made my sister swear to secrecy. I knew if she told on me, or if I went to get help for my hand getting cut, I'd get yelled at for using the box cutter without asking and cutting myself. So I applied pressure until the bleeding stopped and then grabbed some hydrogen peroxide, Neosporin, and a bunch of Band-Aids and dressed my wound.

Wow, I knew at a very young age I'd get yelled at for sustaining an injury. Of course I didn't feel safe telling my parents about my rape.

Over the next few weeks I'd remember bits and pieces about the rape, understanding why I hadn't told anyone.

I had been drinking the night before, and my friend insisted I stay at her place instead of driving home. One of our colleagues from work tagged along, hoping for an after-party.

I woke up the following morning as my head was slamming against the arm rest of the couch I had passed out on the night before. It took me a few moments for me to get my bearings through the haze of a late night, little sleep, and a ripping hangover. The colleague from work had apparently also stayed the night and was on top of me. I had rebuffed him and given him a clear "no" the night before, but I woke up as he was assaulting me.

Afterward, I took Plan B so I wouldn't get pregnant and committed to a lifetime of silence.

For eleven years I didn't tell a soul. After the assault, I didn't report it to the police, I didn't go to the hospital, I didn't tell my friend whose house it happened at. I didn't tell my parents. I just went home, showered, and swore I would take it to the grave.

Girls like me don't get raped.

Work was a toxic battlefield. Every time I went into the kitchen, he was there, leering at me. I freaked out on multiple people, was short with customers, and I found myself acting out, unwilling and unable to articulate what happened to me.

If I told my manager, would he believe me? Would I get fired? Who *would* believe me? If I couldn't tell my parents, who could I tell? Who would be there for me? Who could I trust? A few weeks later after *The Bachelor* revelation, Barry and I were sitting on the couch again.

"Remember when you asked if women don't share stuff because they're afraid of being judged for what happened to them?" I asked, testing the waters.

"Yes," he said.

"Can we talk about something?"

"Of course." He turned off the TV.

I took a deep breath and told him. He held me close as I cried, recalling the details of the most violent thing that had ever happened to my body, mind, and spirit.

I had never longed for a deeper connection with Barry. I had always felt like we were on the same page, even when that was still my deepest, darkest secret. But now that I had finally shared it, I felt free from the weight of it. I had been carrying the trauma silently for more than a decade. I didn't realize what a toll it had taken on my body until I felt the weight release after the words escaped my lips. I had sworn to myself I would die with that secret buried within me, and in that moment, to finally let someone else in, to break down the last wall that I had built up, felt nothing short of revolutionary.

To say that my husband is the most supportive man on the planet is the understatement of the century. As I continued watching clips of his interview portion of the documentary, I was reminded of how lucky I was to share my life with someone like Barry.

We'd been through some heavy times since we'd met. It had never been anything between us, but an onslaught of life events that had happened to us or around us. It was the stuff that, if you aren't committed to growth, if you're afraid of change, or if you can't communicate how you're feeling without fear of judgment, could completely derail a relationship.

I had seen the demise of previous relationships over things that weren't nearly as serious, so it took a lot of faith on my part to know that it was not like those relationships. At the end of the day, each instance that could have ruined us brought us closer together. We figured it out. We always do.

In watching his interview and chatting with the production crew, we discussed how relationship dynamics can change in the face of shocking news. Lifestyle changes can be taxing on a relationship if one of the partners has no desire to change. While I was the one with diabetes, Barry was all in on helping me manage the disease, and he didn't stop there. The fact that Barry was right by my side, applying the changes I was making for my health to *his* life was powerful. I didn't have to worry about different grocery lists, I didn't have to worry about temptation in the fridge or pantry. He was all the way on board. He stopped drinking alcohol when I chose to cut it from my life. He held me accountable. He joined me for the bodyweight exercises in the backyard. We started paddleboarding more frequently. He cheered me on as I continued to lose weight, and he supported me leaving the agency and the six-figure salary that provided for our family in order to prioritize my health. He was all in, which made it much easier for me to be all in.

Having the opportunity to share my story with the team from the media company, in that format, was one of the most powerful experiences of my life. I was able to reclaim parts of my story that I had shied away from, particularly my athletic career. As we made our way to the last location on the final day of filming, I started to visualize what the next chapter of my life would look like.

Our last location was Sunset Cliffs for a sunset shoot. I put on my new jeans and a purple sweater, the same shade of purple that was part of the brand colors for the startup I was joining, and I power posed all over Sunset Cliffs. I envisioned these images gracing magazine covers. The main reason I set the goal of being CMO by thirty-five was so I could grace Forty Under Forty lists and announcements for CMO of the Year. I knew joining the startup was a good choice. I knew I could make a difference there.

TRAIL OF LIFE

If you've been through some hard times and you're here reading these words, congratulations. You are a survivor. Now, if you're here comparing

When I posed for this photo, the life I'm living today wasn't even on my radar.

your story to mine, thinking you've survived more or less, do yourself a favor and stop the comparison game. The hardest thing I've been through and the hardest thing you've been through may be radically different, but that doesn't make them more or less important. Our pain is relative to our experience, and when it comes to trauma, it isn't a competition.

We aren't naturally equipped to know how to handle this, and few of us ever learn how. We have to start treating mental wellness with the same regard we do our physical wellness. Until then, our trauma will continue to manifest as mental and physical diseases, and we will continue to be plagued by things that wouldn't stand a chance of harming us as much as they would if we weren't so afraid to talk about them.

That's the thing about trauma. It's taboo in this society. We demonize it, weaponize it, and it is killing us.

For years I assumed I was broken, that I was the only one feeling these things, experiencing these thoughts. TV shows, movies, books—they all confirmed my brokenness. It wasn't until I started sharing these stories with close friends that I realized that I wasn't alone.

Before I could even think about talking to my friends about it, however, I had to talk to myself about it. I had to get to the point where
I could even admit that I was raped. I had done such a good job of
slut-shaming myself that it took hearing other friends speak about the
most violent moments of their lives before I could even wrap my head
around what happened to me.

I had to reckon with my own shame and denial, my own internalized misogyny, my own prejudices and biases to realize that I was a
victim of a crime. Once I admitted that to myself, then I could start
the transition from being in complete denial to understanding why
what happened to me wasn't my fault. With that came unpacking the
negative self-talk. Once I realized that my struggles with body image,
weight loss, and unhealthy coping mechanisms were beliefs, fears, and
behaviors that I adopted when I was a child, and then later in life in a
state of trauma, I could start to define a life for myself. I could reclaim
my power. I hated the idea of being a victim. Being a survivor felt like
a more accurate description. When I claimed my status as a *survivor*
of sexual assault, I felt like anything was possible. If I could navigate
life in a trauma-induced haze as well as I had for the past twelve years,
what was possible when I had a full understanding of myself? What
was possible when I understood my triggers? What was possible if I
were brave enough to remove myself from the comfort of the struggle?
What was possible if I believed the hype?

Sexual assault isn't the only kind of trauma, and I hope that piece
of trauma isn't in your backpack. I do believe we're all wearing one
of these backpacks, and we're all carrying different things. Maybe in
your pack it's the weight of your lived experience—racism, sexism,
homophobia, transphobia, fatphobia, ableism, and the crimes that stem
from those fears, insecurities, and projections. Maybe you lost a friend,
sibling, loved one, or child to gun violence, or perhaps you survived a
shooting. If you served in the military, you have had to make choices

on behalf of our country that I can't begin to fathom, and the weight of protecting an entire nation is a heavy load to carry. Perhaps it's taking care of your parents or other loved ones. Maybe you witnessed or survived domestic violence. It could be losing a child, loved one, family member, or friend. It could be bullying, narcissistic abuse, fertility troubles, manipulative partners or family members, or hostile work environments with inconsiderate colleagues.

When we kill the stigma that trauma makes us broken, and start to identify trauma as evidence of common ground, we can move mountains. This is a trail we can and should be walking together.

I'm not saying we should celebrate our shared trauma, and we certainly don't want to dwell in it, but at its very core it shows us how similar our struggles are. Since everyone has trauma, and trauma isn't a competition, it should be abundantly clear: We are all more alike than different.

When we start prioritizing our emotional trauma with the same urgency we do for physical trauma, we can make significant shifts in how we see ourselves, show up for ourselves, and how we show up in our communities, both local and global.

You get to define your trauma. You get to claim the parts of your story you've been scared to claim. You get to decide how you show up, how you heal, and how you move forward in this world. I don't get to do that for you. Your family doesn't get to do that for you. Neither do your friends, colleagues, medical professionals, coaches, or teachers. Only you can decide what you're ready to reclaim. Only you can decide what that looks like.

What happened to me wasn't my fault, but my healing is 100 percent my responsibility. Nobody else can do this work for me. Yes, I can get help along the way, and it is important to feel connected to a community that cares, but ultimately I am in charge of if, when, and how I heal. We're all dealing with enough as it is. Outside of our own personal struggles, the world around us feels like it's more divided than ever, and social media makes it easier than ever to connect, but we feel isolated and alone.

Facing what we've been through is painful and incredibly difficult, and it's also a gateway to the next level of healing. When we get to the point where we can face the trauma, then the rest of our lives come into focus. In order to move through this kind of work, we have to pile on loads and loads of forgiveness. First and foremost for ourselves.

So today I want you to repeat after me: "I forgive myself."

I'm still working to forgive myself. I know that it wasn't my fault, that I didn't ask for it, and that the only person responsible for the crime committed that morning was the man who violated my body.

For a long time I had a very narrow understanding of what sexual assault was, so I didn't think that what happened to me was considered sexual assault because it was someone I knew. I thought that because it wasn't with a stranger in an alley with a gun to my head it wasn't rape. It would take me eleven years to feel comfortable telling anyone about the assault, and it would take just as long to learn that eight out of ten survivors of sexual violence were assaulted by someone they know, according to RAINN (Rape, Abuse & Incest National Network).

I have done a *lot* of work around this trauma, and I still run into circumstances, situations, triggers, memories, and people that make me feel like I'm back on the couch, being assaulted. In this society, we are surrounded by sexual assault, yet we all walk around like it doesn't happen. Rape is an epidemic in the United States. Someone is sexually assaulted every sixty-eight seconds (RAINN).

Celebrities, athletes, politicians, business leaders, religious leaders, educators, medical professionals, members of law enforcement and the military—in every cross section of society there are powerful people who have committed this crime and either gotten away with it or gotten very minimal punishment for it. The very folks we are conditioned to trust in our communities are sometimes the ones committing these crimes. And when that happens, we have some confusing feelings to deal with. We see examples every single day of how the world discards survivors. Our bodies and our memories are the crime scenes, we are the evidence, and when it's never the right time to talk about sexual assault, it continues to get swept under the rug.

Forgiving ourselves is the first step.

MINDFUL MILES

Before we jump into these prompts, I want you to show yourself so much love for surviving everything life has thrown your way and for how you've handled it—even if you'd do things differently, given the opportunity. There is no right way to heal from the worst day of your life, so whatever you did to make it to this point was exactly what needed to happen. It is proof of your resilience, strength, and courage.

- How does it feel to say, "I forgive myself for what has happened to me"?

- If you are a survivor of sexual assault, have you come to terms with what happened to you? Have you told someone you trust?

- When you hear the phrase "The choice is yours" or "Everything is a choice," how does that make you feel?

- Are there chapters of your life you'd like to reclaim as your own? Have you lost touch with certain aspects of yourself that you'd like to reintegrate?

NEXT STEPS

Let's face it. Talking about these kinds of topics is still taboo in most of our society. What happens when survivors stand up and speak their truth? They are chastised, bullied, shamed, and some are even driven to suicide. What can we do to swing the pendulum in the other direction?

For survivors: Have you told anyone about what happened to you? Are you like me, walking around with this story for years, just now coming to the realization that what happened to you was, in fact, assault? Wherever you're at in this journey, you are not alone. I mentioned earlier that every sixty-eight seconds someone is sexually assaulted in the United States. This is officially the shittiest club I've ever been a part of, and I hate to welcome you to it, because the club shouldn't exist. But here we are. Every survivor's journey is different. Here are the steps I took to reclaim my story, claim my status as a survivor, and eventually share this with someone:

1. Have the conversation with yourself. If you haven't admitted to yourself that this was assault, you have to start there. We can't heal what we don't claim.

2. Identify someone you trust to share with. It's 100 percent okay if that person is a total stranger on a sexual assault hotline. Sometimes holding eye contact with someone you know while sharing something of this magnitude feels impossible. Sometimes the people we share with don't have a compassionate response to our stories. Resources like RAINN's National Sexual Assault Hotline are available for free, and the people on the other end of the phone are trained to listen, support, and affirm your experience. It can be helpful in relieving the pressure of holding the story, and can be great practice to build your confidence as you start to verbalize the trauma you endured.

3. Give yourself as much love as you possibly can throughout this process, and know that your story is worth sharing, that

you are worthy of support, and that you deserve to live a life free from the weight of what you've experienced. The world may try to tear you down in the process, but if you survived the act itself and everything that has happened since, you can make it through this too. It's not easy. It doesn't happen overnight. But I promise, it does get better.

For supporters: If someone finds the courage to tell you that they have survived sexual violence, your reaction can really dictate their healing journey. When it comes to surviving trauma—particularly sexual assault and domestic violence—our bodies and memories are the evidence. If someone confides in you, please resist the urge to seek answers to your questions and instead center the experience of the survivor. Understand that they have survived the most violent thing that can happen to the human body, short of being murdered. They have overcome societal messaging and a culture that drags survivors through the mud in order to speak up and share this with you. Don't ask about what they were wearing, or where they were, or if they were drinking, on drugs, or otherwise impaired in some way. The most impactful thing you can say is, "I am so sorry that this happened to you. How can I support you?" Acknowledging what they said and expressing empathy for what they have survived is crucial. Asking a survivor how you can support them gives them the opportunity to tell you what they need, if they know. Chances are the survivor might not know how you can support them, and that's okay. If you know you have the emotional capacity to support this person, please do. If you know you are not capable of supporting this person, help them find the resources that can point them in the right direction.

CHAPTER 10

THE BEGINNING OF THE END

Reacting Versus Responding

After the documentary shoot wrapped, my last two weeks at the agency flew by. Before I knew it, Barry was dropping me off at my new office in downtown San Diego for my first day on the job as chief marketing officer at the startup. First I popped into Starbucks across the street. Usually when I went to Starbucks they got my name wrong. Nine times out of ten, I got my cup and it said *Cindy* on it. On that day they got my name right.

A sign of good things to come.

I opened up my banking app and took a screenshot of my bank balance. My business partner told me that we were on track to hit $1 million in revenue that year. While I knew that wouldn't automatically make me a millionaire, I wanted to remember what life was like before I made my first million dollars, whenever that was.

I knew I was in for a wild ride by joining an early-stage startup, but there is no way I could have predicted how bad things were going to get.

I had connected with Brenda, the CEO of the startup, in an online program for women entrepreneurs. The women participating were from all over the country, and Brenda was in San Diego. Our career paths were remarkably similar, and we connected immediately, as she was also a spitfire who didn't pull any punches when it came to sharing her opinions. With blonde hair and piercing blue eyes, combined with her firecracker personality, Brenda turned heads everywhere she went.

We had been chatting online and in group calls for nearly six months before we finally met in person. A bunch of the women who went through the program were gathering for an in-person retreat, and the venue was a quick fifteen-minute drive from where I lived. I was so excited to meet these women, Brenda in particular. That retreat was a whirlwind, but Brenda and I hit it off right away. Some of the sessions weren't so great, and the woo-woo language the speakers used felt fake and forced. Brenda and I just rolled our eyes and laughed.

At one point I went out into the garden to get some air. I needed space. The retreat took place on the one-year anniversary of Adam's death, and I spent my time under the trees, thinking about him. I'd started the online program after the first event for my company Planet Green Socks, the one I'd named in tribute to Adam. And the very last skydiving event I'd coordinated was Adam's memorial, releasing his ashes into the sky.

As if on cue, the winds kicked up and swirled around me. The whole experience was overwhelming; it felt like Adam was sitting on the bench next to me. After I collected my thoughts and wiped the tears from my eyes, I made my way back upstairs to the room I was staying in. Not long after I lay down on the bed, Brenda came in.

"You would not believe the bullshit they're talking about down there," she said, turning on her Valley girl voice. "Did you know, that, like, you should totally have your opt-in happen above the fold on your website because, like, that's where people can see it?"

It was exactly what I needed to take my mind off Adam.

She sat down on the bed and asked me how I was doing. She knew that it was Adam's anniversary. I told her about my experience under the trees, how I started the program wanting to build out the company and tour the United States hosting badass events, and how, since Adam's memorial event, I hadn't really felt the fire for anything, really.

"You know," Brenda said, "if you kill Planet Green Socks, you aren't killing Adam. He's already dead."

It felt like another release. Who was that beautiful angel? How did she know exactly what I needed to hear? How did she know that I was ready to be all the way done with Planet Green Socks, but was feeling shame around the decision?

I started crying again. She held me and told me everything would be okay. I believed her.

Now Brenda and I were working together, and I was excited as I greeted her in our new coworking space. I showed her my Starbucks cup, laughing about how they got my name right. Today was the best day, and we hadn't even begun to save the world together yet. I felt warm all over. I'd finally made it. She was one of the cool kids, and she liked me enough to be friends and to hire me. My middle school self was stoked.

The coworking space had corner offices available for us, some with views of the bay. When I was in my first agency job, I remember telling a friend that within ten years I'd be running my own team in an office in San Diego with views of the bay. I didn't know why I'd said San Diego; I had never even visited the city. When I said that, I surprised myself, because it sounded so outlandish for an entry-level agency employee to be spouting off about leading teams, let alone doing so on the other side of the country in a city she'd never been to.

Holy shit, I made it. Maybe I'm psychic, I thought as we made our way through the office. I had been helping Brenda with her marketing and branding off and on for the year leading up to accepting the offer to join the team full-time. Our first order of business was to launch our seed round of venture capital fundraising. That was my first task—raise $1 million.

I had never done VC fundraising before, but I did all the research I possibly could. We were using a platform that gave us access to investors, and it also let us offer our friends and family the opportunity to invest in the company. I came armed and ready with a marketing plan that would let folks know what we were up to—a fully integrated program that spanned email, social media, friends and family, and press outreach—and I had a few tricks up my sleeve that I was excited to share with her.

We needed to raise at least $175,000 in the first investment campaign to keep what we raised, otherwise it would be returned to the investors. As we discussed where everything was going and who was responsible for what, it was blatantly obvious to me that it was going to be a while before I got to the marketing part of my job. I was a full-time fundraiser, production assistant, supply chain manager, errand runner, and CEO supporter. Only at the bottom of the list of hats I'd be wearing was why I was actually there: to market the products—bath salts, sugar scrubs, facial oils, and the like—and make sure as many people bought them as possible. I knew I'd be responsible for a lot of tasks outside of marketing, but this was feeling more like a cofounder role to me. It felt risky to ask for what I wanted so early in our working relationship, but I'd never know unless I tried.

I told Brenda that I was super excited to be there, and I had no problem wearing multiple hats, but I needed something more. I wanted to have more skin in the game. I asked if I could be considered a cofounder. She told me yes and that we'd talk about what equity changes and salary changes needed to be made after we got through the fundraising.

In the first few weeks we raised $75,000. We had support coming in from some of the most unexpected places. My network jumped in with donations ranging from the $500 minimum up to commitments of $25,000. I had never asked my community for anything in the more than ten years I had been cultivating professional and personal relationships, and I was blown away by their support. Knowing that my contacts were helping us inch closer to our goal in such significant ways made me feel like I was contributing to the business in an impactful way, beyond the skills I brought to the table.

When it rains, it pours, and opportunity was raining down on our company like we could have only dreamed about. Shortly after we launched the seed round, we received two orders totaling more than $70,000 from a national retailer with stores in more than 400 shopping malls in the United States. When Brenda got the purchase order, I thought she was going to pass out.

It was the biggest order we'd ever received, and at that point, we were still doing everything by hand. We purchased bottles from one vendor, labels from another, and labeled all of the products ourselves. We also made all of the products ourselves. We were doing all of that out of her apartment—mostly in the living room, kitchen, and spare bedroom—no more than 500 square feet of working space. We looked at the total number of units ordered: more than 14,000. My eyes must have been the size of dinner plates. It was one of the most exciting days of my life.

It was also the beginning of the end.

We were struggling to find the funds necessary to purchase supplies for the order. I hadn't been paid yet, and I had taken a nearly 50 percent pay cut to pursue the opportunity, so naturally I was a bit panicked. I figured if I could help us get the order filled, then I'd have a chance of getting paid. I offered to put the expenses on my personal credit card, as I had accumulated quite a bit of available credit when I was working at the agency. Brenda was nervous to accept, but I honestly didn't see any other way. As a business, we didn't have access to resources to get that done, and I was so blinded by the lack of paychecks I was receiving, it was truly the only path I could see that would get me paid and not put me at risk of total financial ruin.

After she agreed to let me fund the first order, we ordered all of the supplies. A cool $11,000 later they started rolling in. It was time to get to work.

A typical day looked like this: Drop Barry off at work around 7 a.m., go straight to Brenda's apartment, and get to work. Depending on the needs of that day, we'd make product, label jars, post on social media, promote the seed round, prepare for upcoming pitches to investors, ship out product for online orders, and try to remember to eat. I was pulling eighteen-hour days, taking as many boxes of product home with me as I could to try to get ahead on the next day's deliverables.

The apartment turned into a pressure cooker as time wore on. As boxes full of product ready to be shipped piled up, the available space in the apartment dwindled. Brenda was literally living in her work, and it was starting to take a toll on her.

On the morning she was scheduled to pitch to the largest global network of angel investors, she called me over early. I arrived and she was in the middle of a panic attack, in the fetal position on the couch. Her husband was trying to calm her down, but she wasn't having it. She was crying, screaming, and shaking, I had never seen her like that, and I was concerned for her. I wanted to fix it and make it all go away. When her husband recommended canceling the call, she wailed even louder. I put my hand on her arm and looked her in the eyes. I knew it was a huge moment for the business, and for her personally. I also knew she wasn't going to pull it together in time. The call was in thirty minutes. It was a quick pitch to confirm the network's interest. If they liked what we had to say, they'd send us on a road show to pitch their investor networks around Southern California.

"I've heard you do this pitch a million times. I helped you with the deck. I could do this for you."

She pulled away from me and turned to her husband.

"This is my pitch," she wailed, louder than before. "I don't want her to do it."

Her husband and I locked eyes, and I knew the call wasn't going to happen. We were going to have to reschedule with the folks who would be able to fund the entire round of fundraising if they wanted to.

What was the point of saying yes to me being cofounder if she couldn't let me support her in that very dire time of need? I understood how much work she'd done to get the company to that point. But was that what the rest of the business relationship was going to look like? Did she not trust me? Did she not think I could handle it? If it were me, and it came down to rescheduling the call that could very well change the trajectory of the company or allowing my business partner to facilitate the conversation, I would want to make sure the conversation still happened. But it wasn't my company to run.

"Would you like for me to email them and let them know you aren't feeling well and see if they can reschedule?" I asked.

She looked at me and her eyes softened. She nodded yes.

I was seething with rage.

Well, at least she'll let me communicate with them and let them know it's not happening today. I gritted my teeth as I rage-typed the email.

For the rest of the day, the image of her pulling away from me when I suggested I take the call kept replaying on a loop in my mind. The look in her eyes was a mix of anger, fear, and disgust. It triggered something deep within me, and for the rest of the day, and for every day moving forward, I found myself walking on eggshells around her, afraid she'd break if I said the wrong thing at the wrong time. And frankly, I was afraid I'd break too.

I started having panic attacks after that. I'd usually have at least one per day. Some days I'd have two. Things were moving so fast between the fundraising and filling these big orders, it was all I could do to hang on and stay alive. I noticed my blood sugar readings were trending back to levels I hadn't seen since right after my diagnosis. To try to keep myself sane between tasks, I'd take a lap around the apartment complex. Brenda and I would have walking meetings to help keep the energy moving, because if I was in that apartment for too long, I got cranky and anxious.

I was walking to get lunch for the team, talking to Barry on the phone, when I started getting dizzy. I told him I needed to hang up because I wanted to have both hands free. I kept walking, trying to take deep breaths as I made my way to the restaurant around the corner. I stood about a block away from the restaurant and started texting Brenda to let her know I was having a panic attack and that I needed help. I made my way to the restaurant, told them I was there to pick up food, and that I was having a panic attack and needed a glass of water. I sat down. My chest felt like an elephant was sitting on it, my heart was racing, and I felt completely disconnected from my body.

A few minutes later, Brenda came running into the restaurant. She had sprinted from the apartment, terrified of what she might find. I sat for a bit and collected myself, and then we made our way back to work.

This pattern would continue for the weeks leading up to the shipment of the first order. I would work insane hours, bring product home with me to label late into the night and again in the morning before I got to Brenda's apartment, then spend all day there hopping in to help with production between my fundraising and marketing duties. I'd go for a walk, have a panic attack, and be rendered useless for a bit, then power through to finish what I was doing when the panic attack came on.

After that incident, due to the prevalence of panic attacks we were both having, Brenda and I established a communication process to help us navigate these situations in a healthier way. The plan was to ask for help if you're capable and able to receive, otherwise get out and take care of yourself, and the other person will let you do that. We didn't need to press each other for answers when we were in the middle of a panic attack. We could always come back to whatever was happening later.

The following week the universe dumped another opportunity on us. We were asked to host a sale with one of the largest e-commerce sites in the world. The way it worked was pretty simple. We would tell them how much inventory we had, they'd list it, and when it was gone the sale would be over. We looked at what we had at the warehouse, gave those numbers to the vendor, and launched the sale.

Our products were flying off the digital shelves, and our physical inventory was quickly depleted. Not one to miss out on a revenue opportunity, Brenda made more inventory available even though we didn't have it, and then instructed me to order the supplies for the products we'd need to make to fill the order.

As I was ordering supplies, I realized none of these items would get there on time without significant fees for expedited shipping. Brenda didn't care. The volume was coming in and that was her only focus—sell as many products as possible, strike while the iron is hot, show traction for the investors. I proceeded to rush order supplies, and when our usual vendors were out of what we needed I sought out other options, most of which were more expensive than our usual wholesale vendors. If she said it was okay, I wasn't going to question it. It was her ship. She'd made that abundantly clear around our fundraising pitch conversation. I was just trying to get the huge orders out the door so maybe I could get paid on time.

Even Barry joined us for a day of adding barcodes to products, and swore he'd never help again after he heard how Brenda was talking to me. He said if I wanted to subject myself to that, that was my choice, but to continue to support me in that decision, he needed to never be around her ever again. It felt like I had just woken up from the deepest slumber of my life. I hadn't even registered that the way we were interacting wasn't healthy. I was so busy I didn't have the capacity to establish boundaries or have challenging conversations.

One order was supposed to be picked up the following morning, and we still had hundreds if not thousands of products to create before the truck came to pick up the pallet.

On pickup day, a teammate from my improv class came in at five a.m. and helped me make bath salts and sugar scrubs. We were in the kitchen, furiously dipping jars into buckets of product, trying to make the most efficient assembly line we could while Brenda slept. By 8 a.m., it was abundantly clear that the order was not going out that day.

I was livid. I had been killing myself to get these products done, having panic attacks every day, having friends come join me at 5 a.m., having fights with my husband about how Brenda was conducting herself in front of her employees, and for what? Facial oil?

When Brenda realized we wouldn't have the products packaged on time, she called her assistant and asked her to see if we could get the pickup scheduled for another day. As her assistant navigated the situation, time felt like it stood still, and all I could do was stew in my frustration. Finally we got an update. Apparently we'd had the dates wrong all along. We thought the pallet was being picked up on Thursday, but it wasn't scheduled until the following Monday.

On one hand that was a breath of fresh air, because we'd have time to get the shipment prepared in time. On the other hand my frustration was bubbling up and over. All of the rush fees and extra expenses to get the supplies for this and our other orders done on time had been completely unnecessary.

That was the biggest shit show I had ever been a part of. Things continued to be just as chaotic and pressured, and the final straw came when one of our shipments got damaged in transit, leaking our expensive products, ruining the whole order, and losing us thousands of dollars.

I felt the sensation of a heavy weight on my chest that happens before I have a panic attack. At that point we had five people in the apartment helping with production, plus me, Brenda, her husband popping in and out, and their two dogs. The living room had a very narrow passageway between stacks of finished product, and there were buckets of ingredients in workstations we created between the walkways: a table set up by the couch, the kitchen table, over the stove, over the sink, in the guest bathroom, a table and chairs on the patio, and two more stations in the guest room, which was serving as our office and partial production facility. The apartment felt like it was closing in on us with so many humans working such long hours in such confined spaces.

I grabbed my laptop and said I'd be back in a bit.

Brenda glared at me. She didn't know I was on the verge of losing it.

"I'm about to have a panic attack, and I need to remove myself from this apartment," I said, recalling the communication process we'd established for this exact scenario.

She looked at me, disgusted, as if my oncoming panic attack were a personal slight against her.

I felt the panic attack coming, but the look she gave me made me pause. I needed to wrap things up there. I started stammering, one of my first symptoms other than the elephant-on-chest feeling, updating the teammates on what the status was at the station I had been working. I tried to organize the materials that were on the table to set it up for the next person. I was embarrassed that it was happening, which made me frustrated. When I couldn't communicate clearly I felt ashamed, and everyone else could feel it.

"Get out of here," Brenda hissed.

"I literally just said that's what I'm doing, Brenda. Just let me collect my things."

I could feel her eyes on me, burning into my back as I navigated around and over piles of product. I could feel her frustration building, and she may as well have been tapping her toe.

"What's your deal?" she pressed.

I took a deep breath. We had discussed how we would navigate a situation like this, and pressing the way she just had wasn't part of the plan. I succumbed to my frustration and rage and felt the trauma tornado take over.

"I'm a type 2 diabetic on the verge of financial ruin, Brenda!"

There it was. Every fear I had about the job and my ability to handle it was out there on the table, for every person who was in the room to witness.

I explained that my blood sugar was on the rise, that I was overwhelmed, that I had extended nearly all of my personal credit for these orders, and I still hadn't been reimbursed or paid a paycheck, and on top of all of that, the orders we had been slaving over were either damaged or late. I was alarmed by how quickly everything was melting down, and how little concern there seemed to be for it on her end.

I also said I wouldn't be funding anything else for the company.

The look in her eyes was one I had seen before: a mix of anger, disgust, impatience, and a general air of, "You're a problem that needs to be fixed." I had seen that look in my father's eyes growing up, and that sent me on another spiral, feeling like a little girl getting scolded.

I left shortly after that, feeling physically hot with rage.

Was that the best way for me to advocate for myself? Probably not. But I had never actually articulated my fears or my needs in such a way, and even though it wasn't graceful, I felt proud of myself.

Fortunately I had an outlet. I had been enrolled in improv classes when all of that was going down, and my classmates became my chosen family. I hadn't found a community like that since I was skydiving, and even though things were stressful for me professionally, my social life was a massive source of inspiration.

One night there was a party for the owner where everyone shared how the owner and the community had impacted their lives. I was overwhelmed with emotion. It was so moving. I thought of how many of my friends had died skydiving and the outpouring of similar stories at their memorials showing people's love and appreciation. I wished we were better at sharing these stories with people while they are still alive to hear them.

My improv classmate, the same one who came to help make products for the big orders, saw me crying. She pulled me aside and asked if she could tell me something.

"Of course you can!"

She dragged me outside and gave it to me straight.

"If you want community, if you want what you saw tonight, you already have it here. We love you like that. You don't need the job or the money or any of it to be happy."

That conversation was like a record scratch on the soundtrack of my life and sent me in an entirely new direction. I didn't need a fancy title with the promise of millions of dollars someday, I could go and live my dream, and I could do it right now.

I started crying again. My classmate was often apologizing for her sometimes broken English, since it wasn't her first language. But there was nothing broken about that message.

After that night I knew I had dreams bigger than facial oil, and I couldn't ignore them anymore. I realized my trigger was being in the presence of someone so fearlessly pursuing their dreams and doing whatever it takes to keep that dream alive. I got so spun up when I saw how Brenda went after these big orders because I had been putting my dreams and my health and everything else on the back burner. Once I saw that I couldn't unsee it.

I wanted to make an impact, and I wanted to make it in my own way. If my recommendations there weren't being heeded, it was time for me to go find my dream and chase it.

At that point I'd had nearly a month to reflect on what happened with Brenda, how I reacted, what I'd do differently, and what kind of support I needed moving forward. I realized that I had been seriously triggered, and my default reactions were ones I had absorbed from my father.

I realized that the way I showed up was learned behavior, and I didn't like how I felt when it happened, so I was in the process of unlearning.

As a result, I figured out that when I get stressed it's hard for me to articulate myself clearly. As long as my default reaction was to fly off the handle and overreact, I had to create space for myself to process and feel safe. I also knew that unless I was very specific about what I needed from Brenda to facilitate a productive conversation, I'd likely end up in another situation where I get frustrated, feel shame wash over me, and then move straight into a trauma tornado.

I suggested that she say everything she needed to say, and I'd take notes so I didn't interrupt. When she was done and she felt like she had gotten everything out, then I would reflect on my notes, ask for clarity where I needed it, and then I could respond from that place. For me to arrive at full understanding of what was happening and respond in the way I wanted to show up versus my learned reactions, I needed to have all of the information. Then I would do the same—say my part, uninterrupted, answer questions for clarity, receive Brenda's response. The way we had been communicating up until that point wasn't working, so maybe this would help.

I felt like it made a big difference. It allowed me to really understand what she was saying instead of hearing it through the filters of my trauma and learned responses. I had the chance to hear it, let it sit, arrive at my own conclusions, and respond from that place instead of jumping in and reacting to each thing she said as she said it.

When it came time to talk about the financial side of things, I was firm in my stance. If paying me wasn't going to be a priority, then the funding stopped. I could not simultaneously continue to extend my personal credit to the business while not being paid. I wasn't independently wealthy, and Barry was working a part-time job. I had no savings to speak of. I wouldn't have suggested this arrangement if I'd had reason to believe I wouldn't get paid or reimbursed.

"When shit gets hard, you run," she said.

"That isn't fair, and you know it," I responded.

She went on to tell me that if I really wanted cofounder status, then I should be okay with not getting paid. Everyone else should get paid before the cofounder, she said. At that point, cofounder was a title to make me feel like I had more skin in the game. We hadn't discussed equity changes or what that would look like, as initially promised. Furthermore, it was my credit that had been keeping the company afloat. I was the biggest investor in the company at that point, aside from the money Brenda had spent to start the business.

I asked about division of labor—who was actually in charge of what—and she dodged the question. She started talking about running the numbers and how she actually couldn't afford my salary, despite what she said to get me signed on.

She didn't outright fire me, and I didn't quit, but ultimately it was my choice—keep working and do it for free because she couldn't afford me, or leave the company.

My mind was simultaneously spinning and crystal clear. My intuition was telling me it was time to pack up and figure out what came next, even if I didn't have anything else lined up. But the comment about "when shit gets hard, you run" kept rattling around in my brain, causing me to doubt my intuition. I needed to share this with someone who knew me well enough to guide me through this, but was far enough removed from the situation to be objective. I called my mentor, Aaron, and asked for his take.

He affirmed for me that the situation was as bad as I thought it was, and I was grateful to be seen and heard in that moment. It wasn't a conversation about how I had only been there for ninety-some days and that I should stick it out, nor was it a judgment about how I make poor career choices. In the absence of the judgment I had internalized (and expected) from prior conversations with my father, curiosity once again took the lead and directed me toward a big realization. This was a pivotal point in my career, and my gut instinct was to call Aaron, not my family. Why? Maybe Little Sydney, who'd cut her hand with a box cutter, didn't want to get in trouble. Perhaps Adult Sydney didn't want to let everyone down when what seemed like her golden ticket to wealth, a huge house on the coast, and a casita in the back for her parents were not all they were cracked up to be. More likely, I didn't want to hear about how I had left such an epic career at the agency to join the startup, and now I was a quitter. Either way, Aaron affirmed that it was an opportunity. Everything I had experienced in my life so far, professionally and personally, had set me up for this moment. It became an opportunity to choose me, to trust my gut, to do something I wanted to do, and to do it right then. I didn't know what I was choosing, but I knew I couldn't continue moving at the pace I had been for the startup. It was my time to go all in on myself and trust that no matter what followed, I would figure it out and everything would be okay. The choice was mine.

TRAIL OF LIFE

You might think it's semantics to talk about reacting versus responding, but I assure you, the difference is monumental. A reaction is something that happens without much thought. A response is something you have time to consider.

When we react, we are stepping into learned communication patterns—things we've absorbed from the environment around us. If you've done the work to heal your wounds, your reactions and responses may be very similar. But if you're operating in a state of unresolved trauma, your reactions are rooted in a trauma response. I call these kinds of moments a trauma tornado. Everything starts spinning, the tears behind my eyes feel like a dam ready to give way to the pressure, and it feels like an elephant is sitting on my chest.

When I would have a reaction like this to a person, place, or situation, it felt like what was happening was out of my control, because it was. Before I started to heal my wounds, the time it took to experience a trauma tornado and then identify what triggered it could take weeks, if not months or years. Something would trigger me, I'd have a reaction, and if I were lucky I could pinpoint the trigger. For the longest time I was just experiencing the world in a perpetual state of trauma. Everything was happening to me, against me, in spite of my efforts. In fact, before I started doing this work I didn't realize I was triggered, I just knew I was unhappy.

Once I started doing the work to heal past wounds, I noticed the time between the reaction and identifying the trigger was shortening. I called them my contractions. Instead of months or weeks, it might only take a few days, then a day, then several hours. Now, if I'm paying attention and not caught up in the panic, I can catch the trigger while it's happening, or I can see the trigger before my body automatically reacts, and I'm able to choose how to respond to the situation. It's like watching life in slow motion after so many years of fight-or-flight responses.

When we're able to recognize that we've been triggered out of a place of fear or rooted in past trauma, first let's give ourselves compassion for being triggered. Most triggers are things that are outside of our control, but if you're like me, you want to be good at healing, so you want to have control over your reactions.

First things first. Control what's controllable. What can we actually control in any given situation? How we show up, how we respond or react . . . and that's about it. We can't control how the people in our lives show up (or not), communicate (or not), or their perceptions of us. What other people think about us is out of our control, and it's none of our business.

Second, give yourself compassion for reacting. When you feel that white-hot shame wash over you because you recognize that you would have done things differently if you weren't activated in the moment, let your inner child know that it's okay. If you've been wandering through life completely unaware of your reactions and this is your first light-bulb moment, give yourself a hug. Do something kind for yourself. Remember, sometimes the awareness is the work.

If the concept of reactions and responses is brand new to you, resist the urge to beat yourself up or feel like you've wasted so much of your life living in this state. We don't know what we don't know, but when we know better, we do better. When I was first becoming aware of my tendency to do this, I had to make conscious choices to soothe myself and let go of the guilt I was feeling for how I had been showing up.

DEEPER DIVE

If your mind is swirling with chaotic energy, remembering all the times when this has happened to you, get outside and get in motion. One of the best ways to move through the discomfort of doing this is to get your body in motion so the energy can move. If you feel like you want to cry, let 'er rip. If yelling at the top of your lungs into a pillow or into the wide-open expanse of a natural area, please do. Whatever helps you get this energy out of your body so you can start to heal from this, do it.

Once you've done something with the energy and you come back into your body, think about your highest, most healed, healthiest, well-resourced self. If all your needs were met and you'd done the work to understand what activates you and now had a deep understanding of how to soothe yourself when this happens, would you react that way? No, of course not. So think about how your highest, most evolved, most compassionate self would respond, and if it feels helpful, give yourself a chance to do it over in your head or journal. Think about what happened and practice your grounded response.

Notice what triggered you in the first place. Where are you? Who are you around? What is happening? Where do you feel it in your body? When you're able to scan a situation like this, you can choose how to respond instead of allowing your instincts to take over.

Over the years, I've seen a lot of memes about how we don't have the same threats we used to in early times of the human experience. Have you seen these? The most impactful one I remember seeing compares threats. We aren't being chased by saber-toothed tigers anymore, but the threat is our boss yelling at us. That one helped me wrap my head around what was happening in my body.

Most of the things that have us in fight-or-flight are benign on their own. For me, an off-balance fan with pull strings that are clinking against the glass of the lamp are a trigger. On their own? *Soooo* not scary. But that's what I focused on during my assault—the rhythm of the pull strings clinking on the glass, instead of the violence that was happening to my body. That is what my brain fixated on.

So when we were staying at a friend's house and I heard the clinking, then looked up, my whole body tensed up, my breathing became fast and shallow, and I felt like I was on the brink of a panic attack. Where was I? In a cozy bed, in a safe home, next to my husband, down the hall from people who love and adore me. I was safe. But that fan . . . the last time I saw something like that, I wasn't safe.

If you find yourself feeling this way, like the whole world is about to implode, do a quick environment scan to remind yourself of your (relative) safety. Where are you? Who are you with? Are you in immediate danger? Can you take a few deep breaths?

MINDFUL MILES

As you start unpacking your reactions and responses, I encourage you to tap into forgiveness, compassion, and self-trust once more. We can't change the past, and there isn't much we can control about the future, but when we get clear on who we are and how we process—and acknowledge our growth in this area—the present feels a lot more inviting. Remember, hindsight is twenty-twenty, so don't gaslight yourself. This is an opportunity to reflect on your experiences, understand how you'd show up differently with the awareness you now possess, and integrate what you've learned into your outlook for the future.

- Have you ever had a reaction at work, school, or home that you weren't proud of? Looking back, what would you do differently?

- When was the last time you clearly articulated your needs without fear of what would happen next?

- Have you ever stopped to ask yourself where your reactions come from?

NEXT STEPS

When we are triggered, our nervous system becomes dysregulated. So how do we bring ourselves back into balance? Try grounding, or earthing.

It's as simple as taking off your shoes and socks and walking on the earth with bare feet. Whether it's a sandy beach, a patch of grass, the soft forest floor, or anything in between, if it's outside and natural, it's going to help you. Humans have been wearing shoes for tens of thousands of years, starting as a simple way to protect the soles of the feet from frigid conditions. Throughout the years, the styles have evolved with new technology (like sewing machines). When sneakers became popular in the mid-1900s, we started to separate ourselves from the earth with synthetic materials in the soles of our shoes, disconnecting ourselves from the organism we call home.

Think about it. We wake up on a bed that is not on the ground, we walk on synthetic materials, we put on our shoes to go for a walk or run errands or go to the office, we go to the gym or out for a hike wearing our shoes, then we come home, take our shoes off, put our feet back on the synthetic surfaces, and get back in our ungrounded bed.

Now that science is catching up to ancestral knowledge, it gives language to our modern society that makes sense of this natural earthing. The short version is that when we don't take time to reconnect with the earth, we don't have anywhere to discharge the excess electricity in our bodies. Excess electricity or heat in our body leads to inflammation. Inflammation leads to mental and physical disease. According to studies, grounding appears to improve sleep, normalize the day-night cortisol rhythm, reduce pain, reduce stress, shift the autonomic nervous system from sympathetic toward parasympathetic activation, increase heart-rate variability, speed wound healing, and reduce blood viscosity.

As I look back on how I reversed my diabetes, all of my efforts were centered around reducing inflammation. I didn't consciously look for a nutrition plan that was branded as anti-inflammatory, but as I listened to my body (and checked my glucometer), I naturally came to prioritize foods that contributed to lower blood sugar readings. I didn't get into hiking thinking, Oh, great, this is a super grounding activity, but I felt the magical benefits.

How can you incorporate grounding or earthing into your day? Depending on the climate you live in, this routine will change throughout the seasons, but the easiest way to tap into the benefits of this practice is to simply get your bare feet on the earth. Take an existing part of your daily routine—like drinking tea or coffee, journaling, talking on the phone with a friend or family member—and do it with your feet in the grass. If you go for walks or hikes, find a nice quiet spot on your route to take your shoes off and take in the scenery, barefoot.

CHAPTER 11

HIKING MY FEELINGS

Unpacking Self-Reflection

After ninety-five panic attack–inducing days at the startup, I quit. No backup plan, no savings to speak of, no other jobs lined up.

It was the hardest decision I ever made, and at the same time the easiest decision I ever made.

I needed a reset button. I remembered I still had some unfinished business with the Trans-Catalina Trail, and even if I couldn't walk right for a few weeks after that first hike, I knew it would help me clear my head. Barry and I had promised each other that we would do the whole trail again someday, and I wanted *someday* to be *tomorrow.*

I looked at the calendar and figured we could do our second attempt at the Trans-Catalina Trail for my thirty-third birthday during the first week of June. It was abundantly clear that I needed some nature therapy. That gave me two weeks to train for the hike, and now I had no responsibilities to return to when I got done with that adventure.

Four days after I left the startup, Barry and I went for a hike to Cushi-Pi (the ancestral Kumeyaay name for the mountain that colonizers renamed Stonewall Peak). The hike was in Cuyamaca Rancho State Park, in eastern San Diego County. I was trying out a pair of trail runners for the first time, as opposed to hiking boots, and this was the first hike we had done in a while. The first thirty or so minutes were pretty rough. My chest was congested, and I just wanted to clear it out. My legs were on fire on the initial climb out of the parking area. Even though I had been walking a lot while I was at the startup, those walks were on flat, level ground. As we made our way above the tree line, I saw a railing that would help us get to the summit.

One of the reasons we'd picked this hike was the promise of 360-degree views of San Diego County, but May gray was in full effect. May gray is a result of the marine layer that blankets coastal Southern California in May, which fades into June gloom before opening up to warmer weather and clear skies in July. At the summit, the marine layer was completely blocking the views we were looking forward to, but I had Barry snap a picture anyway. As I watched the squirrels beg for my almonds, I took stock of everything that had happened so far that year. The documentary, leaving the agency, joining the startup then leaving it. At that point, I was actually training for the Trans-Catalina Trail. I had lost sixty pounds since my diabetes diagnosis. Considering I had just left two jobs in the span of five months, I was shocked that I didn't feel more stressed. In fact, I wasn't stressed at all. For the first time in a long time, it felt like I could exhale after figuratively holding my breath for months. And at that moment, on the summit of Cushi-Pi, I could let it all out. So I did.

I thought about the last time I went through something that stressful—the last half of 2014. After Adam died, everything happened so fast. Life felt like tragedy after tragedy, and all I could do was numb myself to cope with it. In 2014, I'd jump into a pint of Ben & Jerry's or a bottle of wine more often than not. But I wasn't deploying my normal coping mechanisms anymore.

So how *was* I coping? Since I'd been diagnosed with diabetes, I'd kicked the ice cream and wine to the curb. I realized I was *hiking* my feelings instead of eating and drinking them. I was pleased with a positive shift and a new coping mechanism, but I couldn't help but wonder: Why had I been eating and drinking my feelings to begin with?

Later that week, Barry and I set out to complete the Mission Trails Regional Park 5-Peak Challenge in one day, which would have us summiting Cowles Mountain, Pyles Peak, Kwaay Paay Peak, and North and South Fortuna Mountains. That would replicate the first day on the Trans-Catalina Trail, and if we could get through it, we could definitely handle the TCT. Physically, I wanted to see what we could handle in a single day. Mentally and emotionally, I wanted to see what would happen for me on the trip in light of the discovery that I had been hiking my feelings.

Cowles Mountain is the most heavily trafficked trail in San Diego, easily accessible from most parts of the city. On the way up I was struggling. It felt like it was taking me way longer than usual to get warmed up. I started to worry about whether I was going to be able to make it all day, as that was the first long hike we'd attempted since I was diagnosed with type 2 diabetes.

Prior to picking hiking back up, I met with my doctor to talk about any concerns I had while preparing for the Trans-Catalina Trail. Initially I was worried about the quality of the food I'd be eating on the trail since the complete overhaul of my nutrition plan postdiagnosis. I knew I needed to consume carbs (and sugar) to keep going on a long backpacking trip, but I didn't fully understand what that meant as a newly diagnosed diabetic. My doctor assured me that it would be fine to eat what I normally pack on hikes, and if anything, I should be more mindful of my sugar levels going too low, since I'd be hiking all day, not too high.

Making our way up Cowles, I was worried about my blood sugar plummeting after hours of activity. I was worried I didn't pack the right snacks. I started to catch my thoughts wandering toward radically unlikely scenarios and stopped to take a breath and a sip of water.

I had to remind myself of how far I've already come (before even setting foot on the trail) and give myself a little of the empathy that I so readily deliver for others.

Sydney, you've lost nearly sixty pounds since you were diagnosed. You are in the best shape you've ever been in. The five-miler you did last week felt like a piece of cake, remember?

As we approached the top, I blurted out to Barry, "I don't think I'm going to be able to do this today if we don't eat between stops," continuing the conversation we'd been having in my head (which was just me freaking out about food by myself). He gently reminded me there was a deli across the street, and the park was surrounded by civilization, and we could *probably* find some food after we completed Cowles and Pyles.

I find that the first fifteen to thirty minutes of any hike is my internal negotiations with myself. At some magical moment my negative self-talk goes away and the bliss I find while hiking returns to me, and I'll shout, "Oh yeah, I love this!" That's usually when Barry turns around and smiles and says, "Yup! We're just walking!" and all is well.

When we got to the summit of Cowles Mountain, I was feeling much better and was excited to take pictures at the summit signs to signify my completion of the peak for the challenge.

From the summit of Cowles we went around to Pyles Peak, where the crowd thinned out. I settled back into my head and got comfy exploring my thoughts again. I thought back to just a few minutes prior, when I was convinced that there wasn't food for me to eat around there and that surely I'd die on the trail not even a few miles into it. I giggled. My brain makes some pretty dramatic jumps sometimes.

I smiled to myself, remembering that I'd be okay throughout the hike, and I could trust that I knew how to take care of myself. When I posted about the challenge on Facebook, I mentioned that Barry thought we could tackle the challenge in one day, and I remembered

Completing the 5-Peak Challenge in Mission Trails Regional Park in one day is a great way to test your endurance and build confidence. It closely mirrors the conditions, distance, and elevation gain on the first day on the Trans-Catalina Trail.

how some people left comments questioning my ability to complete the hike. My pace quickened a bit, as did my breath. I felt a surge of energy of sorts, and though I was still in motion, my attention focused on the feeling. Was it fight or flight? Or was it a surge of motivation? The physical sensations were the same, and if I didn't pause to check in with myself, I very easily could have confused motivation for fear.

I'd be lying if I said there still wasn't a little piece of me that had wanted to prove myself to the folks who assumed I couldn't do the challenge. But that surge of energy I caught in that instance was all for me. I wanted to prove to *myself* that I could. Hold *myself* to my word. Instead of using the energy to flee a scene that didn't need fleeing, what would be possible if I'd directed some of that energy toward caring about my well-being?

I cheered myself on. *You said you wanted to do this in one day. You already bagged one peak, you're halfway up the second, and it's not even 9 a.m. You got this. Keep walking. Go get those summit selfies.*

The hike to the summit of Kwaay Paay was the shortest distance to the summit of the five peaks we were tackling: 2.4 miles. The elevation gain was also the lowest of the segments of the challenge. So when we got there and it was straight up, no switchbacks, with all of the elevation gain at once with no relief from the steep incline, I was taken aback. I started to feel my hip get a little tweaked, like it had on that last summit before Black Jack Campground on the Trans-Catalina Trail. I was wishing I had my trekking poles from the car so I could take a little pressure off. About halfway up, I turned around, took a few deep breaths, and out of nowhere tears started to well up, triggered by memories of being told, "When shit gets hard, you run" on my way out of the startup.

When shit gets hard, you run.

Could I prove that true or false? Taking a look at my career, I thought about my résumé, including bartender, PR executive, competitive skydiver, data analyst, business owner, marketing director, and chief marketing officer of a beauty brand. What did I see? Chaos? Organized exploration?

When we filmed my diabetes documentary, the screening interviews helped me understand my story better. I had been on a journey for the past seven or eight years to figure out who I am and what I'm supposed to be doing on this planet. Professionally, most of the bullet points on my résumé have marketing as the common thread, as that was the role I was serving in each of those industries. But more than that, my résumé was a demonstration of my love of learning. Marketing was something I was good at. I worked on building that skill and exploring how it could be used in a variety of industries.

I've been told that my résumé is both problematic and inspirational, so you can imagine how that might lead a girl to question what she's been doing for the last few years.

The Kwaay Paay section of the trail reminded me that it's 100 percent okay for me to do things my way. My way has historically been to find an activity, get really saturated in it, learn as much as I can and/or acquire a particular level of understanding, and then move on to the next thing.

I truly believe that life is a series of experiences strung together to teach you how to get the most out of the human experience. If you're paying attention, damn near every experience can teach you something about yourself or the world around you.

As I stood facing back toward the parking lot, looking out over the park and the highways in the distance, I just absorbed all of it and let it seep into my bones.

Hiking our way through the grasslands to the Fortuna Saddle Trail for our final two peaks, Barry and I were talking about how much our lives had changed since my diagnosis.

"I could very well run this section," Barry said to me. "I feel like I could do that."

"Me too!" I said.

A few minutes later I chuckled to myself. Barry asked what was so funny.

"I never in my life thought we'd contemplate running together, that's all!"

The Saddle Trail is one very steep fire road that takes you up to the peaks. No shade. Just a wide road with varying amounts of gravel on it, at points so steep it felt like an ice pick would have been helpful to navigate the dramatic incline.

As we were approaching the summit, I felt a little nudge toward understanding. *When you're all talked out, go hiking.*

Over the past few months I had been leaning heavily on my friends and family for support through these transitions. From being an undiagnosed diabetic at my heaviest to the lightest weight I'd ever been as an adult. From corporate life to startup life to this new chapter. I had been talking through a lot of things. I was spending countless hours on the phone working through my feelings, and by the time it was all over, I made the decision to make room for adventure so I could find out what my purpose is. I was all talked out.

But I knew myself, and I knew that just because I was all talked out didn't mean I was totally healed. The hike up to North Fortuna further connected the dots between coping mechanisms and diabetes and brought the concept of hiking my feelings into focus.

After reaching the summit of North Fortuna, we had one peak left to go: South Fortuna. It's usually at that point on any hike where I start wishing we had longer to go because I get so much enjoyment when I'm in motion, processing, and breathing in fresh air. I was thinking back to that morning on Cushi-Pi, revisiting just how much change I had experienced in my life lately.

As Barry says often, the only constant in life is change. I'm a walking example of embracing that, and it's really humbling to look back and see how I'd been resisting it. For most of my adult life, I'd worked in a high-stress career. Public relations is stressful. Marketing is stressful. And doing that in an agency environment or the skydiving industry is additional stress on top of an already stressful career choice. My last chapter at the startup was a lot of new—a new industry, new responsibilities, and an entirely new language to learn as we were trying to navigate the world of venture capital, investors, and scaling the business. Between all that, skydiving, and the new adventure I was embarking on with no real plan in place, clearly I'm not afraid of taking risks.

So why was it then, at almost every turn in my career, I inevitably felt like it just wasn't a good fit? Was it that I'd really internalized the US programming of "Do more, be more, have more"? Was it because I was incapable of being satisfied? Was I wishy-washy?

Or is it possible that I'd been trying to fit a mold I wasn't designed to fit? Just because I'm good at marketing doesn't mean that I need to be doing that exclusively, let alone for the rest of my life. Giving myself permission to sit with that reality was a process of extending myself the same empathy I extend to others.

That was certainly the case for my health. I tried everything under the sun to lose weight before my diagnosis and I could never keep it off. Every time I set out to lose weight, I would ask my skinny friends what they were currently doing. Some of them were on a fad diet, some were combining diet pills, some worked out three hours a day, some just had good luck and good genetics.

Then I would follow the same cycle, every time:

- Try something new.

- Do it obsessively until I saw results.

- See results, be excited by results, reward myself with unhealthy food.

- Never return to the activity that led to the results.

- Gain all the weight back and then some.

If it were possible for me to get diagnosed with diabetes, go to the educational classes at the hospital, review all the things I'd done to get healthy in the past, and throw it all away to instead follow my intuition and see incredible results, then perhaps it was possible that I had been making career choices from a place that was not aligned with what I actually wanted.

Perhaps if I took the same refined approach to my career as I'd taken with my health, I could finally find what I'd been seeking professionally. That was heavy. And like the whole chasing dreams thing at the startup, once I saw it, I couldn't unsee it.

After those first training hikes, the realization that I'd shifted away from eating and drinking my feelings and into *hiking* my feelings felt nothing short of revolutionary for me. I was thankful for how a diabetes diagnosis had reframed my approach to health and wellness. Truthfully, diabetes was the best excuse I ever had to start shifting out of saying yes to things that weren't contributing to my health. Making healthy choices for myself and saying no to the things that could derail my progress was empowering.

Still, while hiking my feelings felt like an interesting container for processing emotions, and while the 5-Peak Challenge was a definite confidence booster to get me physically prepped for my second attempt at the Trans-Catalina Trail, I still hadn't answered the big question of *why* I'd been eating and drinking my feelings to begin with.

I had been doing a lot of journaling around the hiking my feelings idea and started posting my essays on my website, as well as some pictures on Instagram. Suddenly my branding instincts kicked in. Had anyone used that hashtag? Was the URL available? How about the Instagram handles? The hashtag hadn't been used before and the handle was available. So was the URL. I was shocked that someone else hadn't thought of it yet. Of course I wasn't the first person to find healing and clarity on the trail, but it blew my mind that #hikingmyfeelings wasn't already a thing out there in the universe. It felt like a calling.

I was loving having the time to hike whenever I wanted, but those two weeks after I left the startup were a weird limbo space. For the first time in my life I didn't have a backup plan, and I didn't have another job lined up. I found myself obsessively refreshing email I didn't have access to anymore, and would waffle between feeling sad that nobody needed me anymore and elated that I was only responsible for myself.

With all of the hiking and paddleboarding we were doing, Barry and I felt super prepared for our second trek across Catalina Island. I picked up some extra items to keep on me in case my blood sugar went low. I also bought a different pair of shoes for the trip so I could have a bit more grip.

On the day we were scheduled to leave San Diego, we had an easy travel day planned. We got everything packed up the night before. Barry couldn't get out of his opening shift, so it would be an early start for him. We planned on heading up to Long Beach in the afternoon, crashing with our friends again, then we'd wake up, take the 6 a.m. ferry to Avalon, and hit the trail.

We woke up early on travel day, and I dropped Barry off at work. I drove back home and packed up the car with all of our gear. The dogs would be staying home this time, so I wrote a note for the dog sitter and got in the car.

I had been holding on to my work-issued laptop computer as collateral, which was hilarious considering I was owed close to $13,000 and the computer was worth $750. I wanted to get the computer out of my possession before we left. I needed that chapter to be closed so I could go take the first steps of the rest of my life without the energy hanging over my head. I didn't have time to go to Brenda's first. I needed to get

Barry. I picked him up, asked about his day, and went through all the possible things I could say to Brenda as I gave her the computer back. We pulled up to her place, and I walked up to the patio by the gate, just like I had every day I came to work. She came out to greet me, we exchanged awkward small talk, and I mentioned that we were headed to Catalina Island to hike the TCT again.

I handed her the computer and said, "Have a lovely, lovely time."

I walked back to my car. *Smoooooooth, Sydney. What does that even mean? My last words to someone I considered to be one of my best friends were, "Have a lovely, lovely time?" Seriously?* I had played the exchange out in my head and was ready for an epic monologue if the situation called for it. It was so anticlimactic. An unemotional end to an emotionally turbulent chapter of my life. A MacBook Air doesn't weigh much, but the second I handed off that computer I felt lighter. I had a bit more pep in my step. Energetically, the cord was cut. That was the last connection I had to that woman and that business, and I was about to embark on the adventure of a lifetime, with nothing in my way while I was there and nothing to return to when I got done hiking across the island. It was a clean slate, a fresh start, and I was going to take advantage of the opportunity.

I got back in the car, recounted the conversation to Barry, and laughed.

When a movie gets made about our lives, that scene will be so awkward, I thought.

As we pulled onto the freeway, Barry looked at me and smiled. "You ready to have a great time?"

Yes, yes I was.

"Catalina, here we come!" I said, looking out the window at nothing in particular, lost in my own thoughts.

It was time to start a new adventure.

TRAIL OF LIFE

Before my first hike with Barry when we moved to Southern California in 2011, he coaxed me out into the wilderness with a simple promise. He said hiking was exercise that didn't feel like exercise, and the view was always worth the effort. What he said made sense to me at the time, but it wasn't until seven years later that I would have a full-body understanding of what he meant.

Aside from my time on the rowing team at the University of Kansas and the workouts I was doing when I was a competitive skydiver, every attempt to get into a regular routine at the gym was eventually thwarted by my own boredom, insecurities, or both. To be fair, it makes sense. I am more likely to stay committed to something when I'm engaged in the activity and when there's some kind of reward on the other side of the effort I'm putting forth. In college, two-a-days were no big deal, because on the other end of early morning conditioning and after-class water work-outs was the opportunity to compete with my teammates. In skydiving, on the other side of the gym workouts was the promise of more endurance for our ten-jump training days, and anything that would make it easier for me to maximize my time with my team (and thus the investment and sacrifices I was making to be on the team) was A-okay by me.

Outside of rowing and skydiving, my stints at the gym were usually to lose weight, fit into a smaller dress size, or as a reaction to an insult about my appearance that depleted my confidence.

When I started hiking, the reasons why the gym is not my jam started stacking up even higher. Between the lack of natural light and fresh air, a sterile environment, TVs blasting the news and loud music, and folks grunting and dropping weights, the gym is sensory overload in a way that does not feel healing to me in any way, shape, or form. If you are easily overstimulated or if you've survived gun violence or have trauma around loud noises, being in the gym can send your body into a state of fight or flight. Of course you're going to hate going there, even if you love the activities. That doesn't mean you're lazy. That's your body trying to send messages to your brain that there are better ways to get a good workout—ones that don't trigger you.

After the first trek on the TCT and my subsequent diabetes diagnosis, I started with morning walks around my neighborhood, and they quickly became my favorite part of the day. These weren't grand adventures, but it was time that was explicitly for me to spend with myself. I would leave my phone in my pocket and enjoy the birds chirping in the trees, the cute dogs on my way to the canyon, the fresh air. It was both stimulating and calming at the same time.

Once I started hiking regularly, I was excited by the process of finding new trails, and my curiosity was in full force. I was hugging trees, identifying the plants and animals on the trail, and doing research on the first peoples to occupy the lands we were exploring. My childlike wonder and joy took the reins, and I fully immersed myself in these experiences. Everything about hiking was (and still is) exciting, and it's that excitement that kept me engaged.

This awareness around why the trail was more beneficial for me than the gym would not have come as easily (if at all) if I didn't make time to reflect on my experiences. Before I set out for the second hike across Catalina Island, I did a massive freewrite in my journal. I felt like I had a lot I wanted to get out on the pages, a marked difference from earlier points in my life. I didn't journal for several years, and during the hard chapters of my life when I was an expert avoider of feeling my feelings, I didn't journal because writing it down made it real. For some reason, if the thoughts were only swirling around my brain and body, I could manage that. But the second I said it to someone else or wrote it down, I had to deal with it.

Can you relate? Have you tried journaling, gone hard to start, and then fizzled out? If so, take a look back through the journals if you still have them and connect some dots on your Trail of Life. What happened leading up to your last entry? What happened in the days and weeks that followed your last entry? It's entirely possible your life got so awesome that you didn't have time to journal and didn't have anything tough to process. I've certainly been there. But it's also possible that something happened, something that you didn't want to write down or say out loud. If that's the case, don't beat yourself up about it—you aren't bad for not journaling. It can be terrifying to recount the things we've experienced, and it makes complete sense that you would want to protect yourself from further pain. We all have so much going on in our lives. Sometimes avoidance is the only way we survive. Give yourself a big heaping dose of compassion because, whatever happened, the actions you took between then and now have aided in your survival and were incredibly valuable. Since you're still here, and now that you've got some tools in your toolbox, let's dip a toe back into journaling.

If this is all brand new for you, there's no right or wrong way to journal. You can sketch, doodle, write, use stickers and markers—whatever feels good to you. Let's jump right in with some journaling practices that can set you up for success in self-discovery.

MINDFUL MILES

Let's take a moment to explore self-reflection through the beauty of nature. Just like a tranquil lake reflects the surrounding landscape, self-reflection allows us to see our inner landscape more clearly. It's like standing amid a lush forest, where we can witness the growth, observe the shadows, and appreciate the beauty within. Embracing this practice is like basking in the warmth of the sun, providing nourishment and growth to our souls. Take some time to sit by the shores of your thoughts, wander through the wilderness of your emotions, and let nature guide you toward self-discovery and growth. You deserve this beautiful journey!

- If you've tried working out at the gym and haven't been able to stick with it consistently, is it possible that the gym isn't your jam?

- Do you currently have a self-reflection practice?

- If so, what does it look like? How do you feel after you make time to connect life's dots?

- If not, are you willing to start? What has been holding you back from making time to connect life's dots?

DEEPER DIVE

If you are a survivor of any kind of trauma and don't feel safe to self-reflect, I encourage you to find someone you trust or a therapist (if you have access) to help you process and get to a point where self-reflection doesn't feel like a threat to your survival. We're all on different journeys; honor yours.

What are some of your goals? Write them out. What is each goal, and why do you want it? When we get clear on the *what* and *why* behind our goals and desires, I've found that the *how* (how we achieve it) and *who* (who helps us get there) will naturally fall into place.

How do you want to feel in pursuit of your goals? It's one thing to have them, but to really up the ante on your commitment to them, it's helpful to pick a few words that represent how you want to feel while you're in pursuit of the goals and upon accomplishing them. In my big journal entry before my second hike on the Trans-Catalina Trail, I determined how I wanted to feel in this next chapter of my life:

- **Generous:** I wanted to prioritize generosity with my time and talent.

- **Grounded:** I wanted to prioritize feeling grounded.

- **Joyful:** I wanted to prioritize joy. I wanted to say yes more. I wanted to bring joy to others.

NEXT STEPS

Write a journal entry from the future. For the sake of this activity, let's think about a goal you have for yourself with regard to your outdoor pursuits. Maybe you are ready for your first backpacking trip, perhaps you're planning an epic adventure like summiting a big mountain, or perhaps you simply want to start walking a few times a week to get started. In any case, here's how to do it:

1. If you have a date-oriented goal (e.g., you scored permits for Mount Whitney in California for six months from now), pick a date in the future where you've already achieved this goal. If you don't have a trip booked or if you're still training and aren't even sure how to get it done, don't worry about the accuracy of the date.

2. Write from the perspective of having achieved this goal, imagining that all of your needs are met, and you are happy, healthy, safe, and supported.

3. How are you celebrating? Where are you? Who are you with? How is the weather? Are you eating or drinking anything at this celebration? How does it feel? How does your body feel? How do *you* feel?

4. Go into as much detail as you possibly can, tapping into all of your senses. Really visualize yourself at this celebration and get super descriptive.

5. Mark the date of your celebration on your calendar. Add the location of your celebration.

6. Share this activity with a friend. Every so often, when I find myself feeling really lost and unsure of myself, I write an entry like this and call my best friend, Kat. I say, "Hey, I'm future-pulling for a moment," and then we go into it. I tell her about the celebration (which she would be at), and she affirms my future state, congratulating me, asking me how it feels to finally have accomplished this goal, etc. No matter how silly it may feel, the power of shared intention is real, and to have someone who loves you on your side looped in on this dream is like sending a little flare up to the universe, God, unicorns—whatever you believe in—to help it all come together.

CHAPTER 12

HOT SAGE

Integrating Your Experiences

The morning we were due to catch the early ferry to Catalina Island, we overslept, missed the Lyft driver we'd booked, and made a mad dash to the harbor, arriving just in time to go to the restroom and get in line to board the ferry. We scanned the line and didn't see very many backpackers. As if on cue, the guy behind us asked us if we were hiking the TCT.

"Yes, indeed, it's our second time!" I was a walking exclamation point with my early-bird enthusiasm. Everything was exciting.

"When was your first trip?" he asked.

"December 2016, between Christmas and New Year's."

"Ah, yes, the rain event!" he said, referring to the downpour we experienced that second night in Little Harbor.

Barry and I both laughed.

"Yeah, that was brutal," Barry said.

The guy behind us continued, "Well, they've made some changes to the trail since then: more shade structures, more restrooms, and some rerouting at different points along the trail."

He introduced himself as an employee of the Catalina Island Company, the parent company for everything on the island as far as hospitality was concerned. We chatted for a few more minutes, and a big group of backpackers got in line behind us. Our new friend let us know that REI hosts a Trans-Catalina Trail trip, and he said it was super luxurious as far as backpacking went. They did the trail in three days versus our six-night itinerary, but they set up your camp for you, cook your meals for you, and haul your gear. All you have to do is walk and carry a daypack with snacks and water. That made the experience accessible for newbies who might not have all the camping gear or who couldn't carry thirty-plus pounds on their backs.

Well, that sounds like the perfect environment for hiking my feelings.

The line started to move; it was time to go.

"Enjoy your hike!" he said as we started to board the ferry.

Once on board, Barry and I dropped off our packs and made our way to the back deck. The sun was starting to rise, and we wanted to get some good pictures on the way into the harbor at Avalon.

We got to the island, and the buzz was the same. We grabbed our backpacks, started making our way through town, and tried not to get lost this time.

We passed the mile one marker by the golf course when we heard someone shouting. There was a golfer on the green asking us what we were doing with the backpacks. We informed him that we were hiking across the island, and he was floored.

"Wait, what? You can hike across the whole island? You've inspired me; I'm going to do that!" he shouted at us from the other side of the fence.

I looked at Barry and laughed. "*Baaaaabe,* we're inspiring! What else is possible here?"

We made our way past the golf course to Hermit Gulch, the campground at the start of the trail. We double-checked water, put on sunscreen, moved snacks around to be easily accessible, and went to the bathroom. I grabbed a Planet Green Socks sticker and put it on the trash can.

I tapped into the calm of the ocean as we crossed the channel toward Catalina Island.

Adam is with us on this trip too.

I checked my blood sugar, and it was a bit higher than I'd have liked for it to be at that hour, but with all the stress that morning, to be expected. After I put my glucometer back in my bag, we geared up again and started making our way out of Hermit Gulch. It was a gorgeous day, mid-sixties at the start of the hike, with temperatures forecasted to be in the mid-seventies to low eighties all week. Not a drop of rain in sight.

I paused to take a sip of water and look around. *This spot looks really familiar.* I closed my eyes and opened them again. *Yep, this is the place where I had to tape up my hot spot on the first trip.* I thought for sure it was at least an hour and a half or two hours before I had to pull over last time. Now that I had a bit more experience with the hiking thing, I pulled out my tracking app.

Distance: 0.25 miles

I called ahead to Barry.

"Babe! This is where I had to pull over last time! Guess how far we are!"

Silence.

"We're a quarter mile in!"

I heard laughter and could see him shaking his head.

I had asked myself before we started the journey, "What would be possible if the hike itself wasn't the hard part?"

I was starting to think maybe I was psychic after all.

We kept trucking up the switchbacks and made it to the first shade structure.

I looked at Barry as he took his pack off.

He's lost weight. He looks incredible. He's like a billy goat up these switchbacks, and I'm keeping up just fine. This is a different hike, that's for sure.

We sucked down water, and I reapplied sunscreen and busted out my DSLR. I didn't want my camera to become the tarot cards of the first trip, so I took it out and snapped pictures every chance I could.

We packed it up and kept going. The stretch after the first shade structure was mostly flat, but I knew what was coming. On the flat parts of the trail the hiking was quiet and mindless, just the way I liked it. It was a beautiful day for hiking: the sun was shining, birds were singing, a nice light breeze was blowing when we came around the bend to face the ocean. Life was good. As we passed the place where I took that first full-body picture on the first trip, I started crying. We made our way through the gate that warns you about bison territory and descended into a canyon with fields of sage as far as the eye could see. I remembered that section from the first hike, and as we made our way farther into the canyon as the day wore on, the plants started to heat up. Every once in a while I'd catch a breeze and, with it, a whiff of sage.

"Babe! It smells like sage! Like hot sage!" I shouted ahead to Barry.

After a nice cruise through some of the canyon floor, we started to climb out of that canyon and into the next. As we did, Barry shouted back to me, "Shifting down a gear!"

He said that every time the trail got steeper. It's one of my favorite things and also it drives me crazy. It's my favorite because he does it and it's adorable, and I always pretend I'm driving a stick shift and gesture as if I'm shifting down. It drives me crazy because he's usually a good bit ahead of me, and I could be in the middle of feeling really awesome, but the second the idea of a steeper climb enters my awareness, my whole body slumps a bit. In that case, when he called back, I was already stopped. I had my hands on my knees, silently screaming as tears were pouring down my face.

After smelling the sage, I'd gone down a rabbit hole.

It smelled delicious and potent. My brain made the jump to my uncle Mike, who died in 2014. He used to split his time between New York and San Francisco, and for the holidays, sometimes he'd come

The first day on the trail is full of views like this between hot and dusty canyons.

back to Kansas and surprise everyone. On one particular Christmas, Mike was staying with us at our house. He took over my sister's room, and when he left, it reeked of clove cigarettes. I thought it was so rude that he'd smoke in the house, but Dad later told us that he was smoking cannabis and that the clove masked the smell. I followed that memory as far as it would go—all of Mike's business ventures, his creativity, his spirit, his singing voice.

I hadn't really had a chance to properly grieve his death. He was a ward of the state and died in a hospice house. There was no funeral. My aunt got his remains and sent some of them to my dad in an aluminum, resealable Coca-Cola bottle. That was it. That beautiful bright light was reduced to ashes in a soda bottle.

I thought of all the times Mike's creativity was spoken of in a negative way. For most of my adult life, my father had referred to my uncle as a beacon of hope for the gay community, while also reminding us to go to college, get degrees, and get real jobs. That a life of creativity and performing wasn't going to make us happy because we wouldn't have money. It's almost like we were supposed to embody Mike's spirit but cut our creativity off at the knees.

I looked up at Barry, still bent over with my hands on my knees.

I waved, signaling I was okay. By now Barry was aware of what could happen with me on the trail. He'd seen it before. I reassured him I was fine and told him not to wait for me, that I needed a minute. He kept going, and I stayed where I was. I let it all out. I'd had a similar experience on the first trek across the island, but this one felt more like an exorcism than anything I had control over. Screaming silently, with nothing coming out, like when I was in the shower during a panic attack. Like when we found out Chris had died and I crumpled up on the kitchen floor, and later when we found out he'd killed himself. It felt like when I finally heard back about Adam and got confirmation that he was dead. Standing bent over on the trail, it felt like I was having an out-of-body experience, remembering where I was when I found out all of our friends had died. On an elliptical machine at LA Fitness for Jonathan. Driving when we got the text about Stephanie. Reeling from Graham's death when we found out Tom died. At the skydiving center when they found Marius. Standing near the airplanes when Ken died. At dinner when Larry died. Sitting on the steps when we heard about Avishai. Blow after blow after blow.

As I resumed hiking, I also thought back to the twenty-three friends who died in the four years I was a skydiver. What was my favorite memory with them? What did they mean to me? How could I keep their legacy alive? I spent most of my time looking at the ground, picking my head up every so often to see what was coming and making sure I could still see Barry. For miles, I hiked and processed and remembered and cried and threw up and dry heaved and laughed and bent over, like I had earlier, silently screaming with my head between my knees, as if braced for impact.

When I looked up again, I saw the playground coming into view. Our halfway point.

I picked up the pace to catch up to Barry, feeling lighter in my shoes. When we got to the playground, I slung my pack off my shoulders and grabbed my glucometer from the top pocket. My blood sugar had been a little elevated earlier. I had been concerned about my nutrition and hydration for the trip, and that was the first time I checked my blood since we got on the trail.

I unzipped my glucometer, picked a test strip out of the container, and inserted it into the top of the device. While it turned on, I took the finger-pricking component, put my thumb on the button that cocks the lancet, drew it back until it clicked, and pricked my finger. The blood had no trouble coming through the skin; I was bleeding like a stuck pig. I put a drop on the test strip and closed my eyes.

Please be good, please be good, please be good. It would be so nice not to have to worry about my blood sugar on this trip.

My reading came back. It was perfect. I breathed a sigh of relief and showed Barry.

"That's great, baby! Congratulations!"

I turned off the glucometer, put it back in its case, and put the case back in my bag. I took off my shirt, disconnected my water bladder from my backpack, and made my way over to the faucet to fill it up.

Last time we'd been there, it was just me and Barry. I'd gotten on the swings and done everything I could to delay so I could cool down and give my legs a rest. This time I felt incredible. I skipped over to the water fountain and started filling up my bladder. Behind me was a group of people. As I filled up my water, it hit me.

I was standing at the faucet in my trail runners, trekking tights, a sports bra, and no shirt.

Sydney Williams doesn't run around with her shirt off. I may have been a cheerleader, gymnast, athlete, but my stomach is the part of my body that I was most self-conscious about, the part of my body that was always covered up. What was happening? I felt like I must have blacked out after the good blood sugar reading, because there I was in all of my shirtless glory, feeling the breeze blow across the skin on my bare belly for possibly the first time in my entire life.

It was such a strange sensation, to feel my body cooling down naturally. As the breeze caressed my sweaty back, I felt chills run up and down my spine.

I made my way over to where we'd dropped our stuff, put my bladder back in my bag, and went to sit on a bench to consider what had just happened.

Okay, so no blisters; that's good. Blood sugar is on point. Water is full. I cried a lot back there. Sitting here I feel lighter; I've got some extra pep in my step. I'm not wearing a shirt and I'm not running to hide my body or cover up. How is that possible?

I thought of all the things I'd said no to, for fear of my body being seen: my high school reunion; fun trips to the beach; wearing clothes appropriate for the weather or season, shorts and tank tops specifically.

Yes, I lost weight, but I don't think that's it. Last time I was here it was just me and Barry; there's no reason I shouldn't have taken off my shirt then, but I didn't.

I wasn't sure what was happening, but I was eager to get to the campground so I could write some more and see if I could connect the dots. Barry didn't have to tap his imaginary wristwatch this time. As soon as I finished some of my electrolyte chews, I geared up and we hit the trail again.

I knew we had at least one more big climb, the one where I had to stop every four steps on our last hike on the island. Instead of being discouraged and wanting to avoid a difficult experience, I was looking forward to it. I wanted to see how different it felt compared to last time. We hiked through more sage fields, took a break in the one shady spot on that portion of the trail to suck down more water, and before I knew it, we were looking up at the last tough climb.

Last time we'd done that section of the trail we'd been passed by people we had never seen on the hike before. This time we knew we were ahead of the group we ran into at the playground, but we hadn't seen anyone else yet.

I looked at the hill, checked my shoelaces, and made sure my gear was comfortable. It was go time.

I made my way up the last switchbacks, remembering how last time I was dragging my leg and literally chanting "right foot, left foot."

I started out a bit aggressively, thinking I could maintain that pace. I was wrong. I slowed down and remembered how I wanted to feel on the trip: generous, grounded, joyful.

"Generous," I said, taking a step. In the next chapter of my life, I wanted to feel generous with my time and talent.

"Grounded," I said, taking another step. I wanted to prioritize feeling grounded. What helped me achieve that sense of calm that I so desired in my life?

"Joyful," I said, taking another step. I wanted to prioritize joy. I wanted to say yes more. I wanted to bring joy to others.

This time I could take about ten to twelve steps before I needed to pause and catch my breath, a marked improvement over the three to four steps I could previously take before I felt like I was going to vomit.

I kept my mantra going, even after the hard part was over.

Generous. Grounded. Joyful.

Generous. Grounded. Joyful.

I could see the campground. I was so hot, I was ready to take my shirt off again, put my head under the faucet at the campsite, and cool all the way down.

When I saw our campsite, I started skipping.

I can go to the bathroom! I can eat! I'm so excited to sleep! I wonder what time it is!

We slung our packs off our shoulders and onto the bench of the picnic table. I grabbed my Nalgene and chugged it. When I finished, I took my phone out of my pocket and paused my tracking app.

"Babe, we got here two hours faster than we did last time!" I called over to Barry as he was unpacking his food options.

"Oh, hell yes!" Barry exclaimed, running over to me for a high five.

I busted out my miniature journal and grabbed my phone. I wanted to jot down the details of today before I forgot.

I had brought a pocket-sized Moleskine notebook to keep notes in, versus the big clunky journal I'd brought last time. On the previous trip, I was trying to do big, long journal entries and it started to feel like more of a burden in the moment, so I stopped. I wished I had kept better notes of that first trip, so for this trip I switched it up. At the bare minimum, I wanted to take notes on what I experienced, so I answered the same questions every day. If I felt like writing more, awesome; if not, totally fine, but I'd take note of the following things:

- Statistics for the day: distance, time on-trail, blood sugar readings, calories burned.

- What were my biggest wins?

- What lesson(s) did I learn?

- What am I thankful for?

- How am I feeling right now (physically, emotionally, spiritually)?

- What did I see/hear?

- Did anything stand out?

- Did I use any specific mantras today?

TCT Journal Entry
June 2, 2018
Steps: 28,741
Miles: 11.16 on MapMyRun
Time: 7 hours
Calories burned: 4,329
Bison: Saw 2 en route to Black Jack

@Black Jack!
We arrived almost two hours earlier than last time, holy shit. The last two summits before BJC were INSANE still, but I'm in way better condition upon arrival than I was last time. Bringing my DSLR was a good choice. Tomorrow is my 33rd birthday, holy poop! Today I repeated how I wanted to feel with my steps: Generous. Grounded. Joyful. So far, so good! Having chicken & dumplings for dinner, yay! Let's eat!

BIGGEST WINS: Shaved two hours off our time, feel freaking great, mostly happy tears today.

LESSONS LEARNED: My stories are mine to tell. Tell them, stop comparing or worrying.

THANKFUL FOR: That this is something Barry and I can share. We are so lucky.

HOW AM I FEELING: Grounded. Toes are sore, but not nearly the shit show we had last time. Back is a bit sore. Mentally, incredible. I love being out here.

WHAT DID I SEE/HEAR: At one point I accessed pure joy and bliss. All the sounds disappeared, and I was warm and free and sobbing. Did I die?

WHAT STOOD OUT: How much easier it is this time.

MANTRAS:

Generous. Grounded. Joyful.
I can do hard things.
Get it together, Williams!
HOT SAGE!

I closed the journal and tucked it back into my backpack. Barry was done boiling water for his dinner, so now it was my turn. Chicken and dumplings. A Black Jack tradition for me at that point.

I scarfed down dinner and grabbed my camera to wander around the campground. The way the light was peeking through the trees up near the bathrooms caught my eye, and I found myself skip-sprinting up the hill with my camera to try to get the shot before the light changed. Last time we'd been there, I couldn't even get up the hill to go to the bathroom. I made it up to the top of the hill and started taking pictures of a dead tree that was perfectly aligned with the Trans-Catalina Trail sign. I paused for a minute and just took a good, slow look around. I wanted to remember every detail of the place, of the whole trip. I thought back to the pure bliss state that I found on the trail. I found that place after we left the playground, before we started that last climb. I noted the shift in my mindset.

After I cried so hard I felt lighter.

When I was filling up my water bladder I felt confident.

And on that last climb before Black Jack I felt inspired.

What was happening? And what would tomorrow bring?

TRAIL OF LIFE

The first big piece of trauma I pulled out of my trauma pack on this trip was the grief that I hadn't processed for my friends who had passed. I held that heavy pain in my hands, gave it the attention it deserved, and left it out on the trail. What I put back in my pack was positive memories, their legacy, and my commitment to sharing their stories whenever I could to keep their spirits alive. Once I cleared the heavy stuff, I felt lighter in my mind, body, and spirit. The trail gave me time and space to hear what needed healing and integrate the lessons I had picked up in various books, programs, and my own self-reflection practice. It was only after this unpacking, releasing, and replacing negative memories with positive ones that I was able to take off my shirt at that playground in the middle of nowhere, choosing to cool down naturally versus being unnecessarily uncomfortable yet again.

What can you unpack to lighten your load? At the beginning of this book, I encouraged you to make notes in the margins or a journal when you had a reaction to any of the stories I share here, providing answers to these questions:

- What am I feeling right now?

- Where do I feel it in my body?

- Can I remember the last time I felt this way? What caused the feeling then?

Have you made these notes? If so, go back and review them and see if you can connect the dots. Are you noticing any patterns about how your feelings manifest as physical sensations? When you think about the last time you felt this way, are you noticing any trends?

If you haven't been taking notes, I encourage you to start. This is one of the best ways to reestablish and strengthen the connection between your mind and body. Once you start to identify the patterns, you can start to associate physical sensations with those specific memories (also known as triggers). As you continue to hone this practice, you'll feel the feeling in your body, and you can scan your triggers: What caused this feeling? The time between feeling the feeling or having the experience and naming the trigger may be days, months, weeks, or even years to start. As you continue to practice awareness around emotions and their physical manifestations, the time between feeling the thing and identifying the trigger will get shorter and shorter. You might not ever not be triggered, but at least you'll know it's a trigger, not an actual threat to your safety.

If this is your first time doing something like this, it might feel tedious to keep exploring everything that comes up, especially if you

All smiles at Black Jack Campground, connecting the dots between my inner and outer wilderness.

have a lot going on. I invite you to stick with it, and here's why. This work is worth the effort. We're all carrying different things in our trauma packs, but one thing is universally true with everyone I've ever worked with in any of our programs and retreats at Hiking My Feelings: After the resistance comes flow. And one of the first indicators to me that I had found flow happened on the trail.

I don't have a scientific measurement of how much work you'll have to do to get to this point, because this is your journey and your story. But if your experience is anything like mine or the thousands of people I've facilitated these experiences for, at some point you're going to stop viewing your thoughts, body, and self as some problem to be fixed, and you'll be able to feel how you fit in the giant ecosystem that is every living thing on this planet.

In the context of outer wilderness and inner wilderness, this is how I knew I was successfully integrating these experiences: I started to see myself in the plants and animals around me.

Using Catalina Island as an example, when I got fussy or irritated on the trail, I thought about cactus. Passing through massive patches and entire hillsides covered in prickly pear cactus, I couldn't help but connect the dots. What are the things that irritate me? What makes me feel prickly? When I would come up and over a ridgeline on yet another aggressive climb to sweeping ocean views and a beautiful breeze, I thought about how this trail was imitating life. Every time I thought I'd gotten to the top of the mountain, every time I thought I had healed something, every time I pulled a new piece of trauma out of my trauma pack to process it, it felt like I was standing at the top of a mountain, that I had reached the end. But like hiking, life has ups and downs. You don't get to the top of Healed Mountain and live there for the rest of your life, but the views from that healed place after that grueling climb sure are worth the effort.

MINDFUL MILES

When we're moving at the speed that society expects instead of tuning in to our natural rhythms, we can get lost. If we don't make time to reflect on the experiences we're having, we rob ourselves of the opportunity to extract insights and integrate the learnings into other areas of our lives. Let's take some time to reflect on our journey together through this book so far:

- What are some of the notes you've made in the margins? Have you identified any patterns?

- How does it feel to be doing these practices outdoors?

- Have you noticed how the outer wilderness and your inner wilderness are related?

NEXT STEPS

The questions I asked myself every evening on the trail also apply to daily life. So I suggest that you follow in my footsteps, grab a journal or notebook, and answer these questions every day for at least a week. If you prefer writing in the morning, start by reflecting on the previous day. Alternatively, if your mornings are unpredictable, reflecting in this way before bed is a great way to clear your mind.

1. Measure what matters. What are you measuring on a daily basis? Are you counting steps? Confirming you took all your medications? Do you have a daily meditation practice? Determine what statistics are important for you to document and include them here.

2. What were your biggest wins?

3. What lesson(s) did you learn?

4. What are you thankful for right now?

5. How are you feeling right now?

6. What did you see/hear?

7. Did anything stand out?

8. Did you use any specific mantras today?

CHAPTER 13

YOU'VE ALREADY GOT A BIKINI BODY

Unpacking Expectations and Beliefs

I had never cowboy camped before, and I woke up for day two on the TCT super-refreshed. It was my birthday, and the plan was to stop at the airport to grab something to eat and make our way down to Little Harbor, where we'd celebrate my birthday that night and the whole next day on our day off.

As the sun rose and Barry started to make breakfast, I grabbed my camera and started wandering around the campsite.

"Sydney, turn around," Barry shout-whispered at me.

I didn't know what to expect, and I wasn't sure I'd heard him right. He motioned for me to turn around.

I turned around and there it was: a bison, no more than seventy-five feet away from us on the opposite side of the trail that led up to the campground.

I had my camera in my hand, so I zoomed in as far as I could and took some pictures. I was so still and so quiet that the shutter on my camera sounded like thunder. I didn't want to spook him, so I slowly lowered my camera and tried to make picture memories in my mind.

This bison came through Black Jack to wish me a happy birthday.

I watched as he grazed on the grasses and moved toward a patch of vegetation and trees near the restrooms.

Once he was out of sight, I turned back to Barry and said, "Happy birthday to me!"

Birthday breakfast with bison at Black Jack, I thought, giggling to myself.

We finished our breakfast and packed up camp, heading toward Little Harbor. As we rounded the corner from the bathroom to get back on the trail, we saw the bison again. He was just off the side of the trail, maybe thirty feet from us. We moved off to our left, taking a wide route off the trail to give him plenty of space. Once the coast was clear, we got back on the trail and started laughing.

"Was that the same bison?" I asked Barry.

"Yup! Don't say I never got ya nothin' for your birthday!"

We made our way out of Black Jack Campground and descended into the canyon that separates Black Jack from the Airport in the Sky. I remembered that part of the hike was brutal last time because my toes kept squishing into the front of my boots, making me wince with each step. This time felt like a normal hike, and as we passed the TCT sign on our way into the heavily wooded part of the trail, I posed by the sign with both hands showing three fingers for thirty-three years old. Happy birthday to me!

We started climbing out of the canyon before the airport, passing the soapstone quarry.

Good lord, I was so out of shape last time. How did we get as far as we did without dying or getting seriously injured?

As we rolled into the airport, I felt my stomach grumble.

Oh no, not again. I was thinking about the literal shitstorm that happened last time I ate there.

As I looked at the menu, it was a hard pass on the bison burger, so I went with a BLT with avocado. It was perfect. I'd heard wild things about the cookies at the airport, so I picked one up to have for my birthday

Spending my thirty-third birthday on the Trans-Catalina Trail was one of the best gifts I've ever given myself.

dessert after dinner when we got to Little Harbor. We knew Sheep Chute Road was coming so we didn't waste any time. As we passed the areas where I had to take an emergency poop before, I was so thankful that I was feeling good. We were cruising and making really good time when we came up on the group we had seen the day before. Were they at the airport when we were there? Did they bypass it? Did they start earlier than we did? I didn't remember seeing them at the campground in the morning, and I definitely didn't see them at the airport. We turned toward Sheep Chute Road and the guide called out to us.

"Hey, if you're doing the TCT, the trail has changed!"

I stopped and turned around, walking back toward him. Barry pulled out the map.

They were right. Sheep Chute Road wasn't part of the TCT anymore. Instead of getting curious about the trail change or feeling grateful that we didn't have to relive the brutality of Sheep Chute Road, I felt a pang of panic. I didn't know what was ahead. As challenging as it was last time, I was prepared for Sheep Chute. Was the new section going to be harder?

"Pass us here, and around that corner you'll see a sign for Big Springs Ridge Trail. Can't miss it."

We thanked them and kept hiking. My panic heightened. *What will this section be like? Why didn't I look at the map after that guy said the trail changed? Shit.*

I took a deep breath. *Everything is okay.* I was hot and out of breath and feeling a bit anxious. I had packed a cooling towel and that sounded like exactly what the doctor ordered. I took off my hat, draped the damp towel over my head, and put my hat back on. As the breeze whipped around my neck, it felt like personal air conditioning.

"Oh, wow that's so much better," I sighed.

"Total game changer!" Barry shouted, his towel in a similar configuration.

We found Big Springs Ridge Trail, and I asked Barry to take a picture of me by the sign. As I looked ahead to the trail, I could see where Little Harbor was hiding in the marine layer. The trail itself was a gorgeous single track, cut into the side of the mountain. I saw the grass swaying before I felt the breeze pass through the towel, cooling me down again.

"Oh shit, I could get used to this!" I cheered as we started hiking.

Everything was gorgeous. Actual single track, not deeply eroded fire roads. A hiker-friendly descent into Little Harbor, not a super aggressive road that jacked Barry's knees so good last time that he had to take the trail walking backward. It was hiking luxury. I felt like Julie Andrews in *The Sound of Music*.

We continued through grassy mountainside, over some exposed rock, and crested the final hill before our descent into the campground. I could see Little Harbor, Whale's Tail Rock, and Shark Harbor. We passed through rock piles and cairns, and I watched the marine layer burn off before my very eyes.

We're making incredible time.

Resisting every urge to spin around like Julie Andrews on this grassy hillside.

The campground started to come into view, and we could see the campsite we were at last time during the rainstorm. I was a good distance behind Barry. I was overcome with gratitude for how much better the hike was feeling, and I was peaceful in my state of moving meditation. I heard Barry shout something, breaking my daze, so I picked up my pace to catch him. As I came up behind him, he started singing "Happy Birthday." I started crying.

We wandered around the campground and realized we were on the lower campground, closer to the beach. I was so stoked. It was the best birthday ever; I woke up, took some awesome photos, saw a bison for my birthday breakfast, saw the bison again on our way out of the campground, got a BLTA, didn't shit myself, and the new section of trail was delightful. What else was possible? This was a dream!

We found our campsite and assessed the sleeping situation. We hadn't brought the tent, but given how close we were to the ocean, we knew we didn't want to wake up all moist from the sea breeze. Barry made a lean-to-style tent, stringing the tarp up between trekking poles.

Ugh, I love seeing this man in his element, I thought. *So sexy!*

The hike into Little Harbor was a quick one compared to the first day on the trail, so we had plenty of daylight to kill. I set up the solar panel on the picnic table, plugged it into the portable battery to charge it up, and changed into my bikini. Time to get some pictures.

Walking down to the beach, I thought of all the times I had wanted to be at a beach in a bikini but didn't feel comfortable enough to enjoy it. I had spent so much time covered up after the assault that buying that one-piece and loving myself in it was such a shift. Now my favorite, perfect one-piece didn't fit anymore. It was too long for me, and the crotch of the suit hung below my actual crotch.

Buying the bikini had been a totally different ball game. I'd gone in knowing exactly what I wanted: something sporty that was both cute and practical for paddleboarding and being active in the water.

Looking through the rack, I'd grabbed a large and medium first. I put the large on and it was too big.

Wow, I have lost weight.

I slid into the mediums and turned away from the mirror. My butt, as I knew it, had left the building. Where my juicy cheeks used to live, pancakes now resided.

I need to build a new butt, I'd thought, chuckling to myself.

Not judging, no hatred, just observations about my new body. It felt like the first time I'd been in the dressing room. Once again, I hadn't recognized my body. Once again, I was curious about how I'd gotten there. I knew I had been working hard, managing diabetes via a complete lifestyle change, and the weight had melted off quickly.

I looked at myself, noting the parts of my body that were different. My arms were more toned, as was my back, thanks to paddleboarding. My legs were much thinner and starting to develop some definition, and was that, wait . . . no, it couldn't be. My thighs weren't rubbing together anymore. *Do I have a thigh gap?* My mind went into overdrive.

Where are the free drinks?

Do I get more signatures in my yearbook?

Will Stephen (my middle school crush) pay attention to me now?

Are there men beating down the door to come ask me on a date?

Who are these fellas? Can't they see I'm off the market?

Versions of me at twelve, sixteen, eighteen, twenty-one, and twenty-eight all had questions.

There I was, thin enough by my own standards to feel confident enough to buy a bikini. For the first time in a long time, I hadn't talked myself out of it. So Little Sydney was cautious to celebrate. She wanted to make sure the universe delivered on the other promises that we chased every time we set out on a weight-loss mission.

Thin girls get more friends and more yearbook signatures.

Thin girls get free drinks.

And lots of dates.

And a husband.

I broke the news to Little Sydney and assured her that we were doing just fine in all of those departments, and the only thing that mattered was that we were happy, healthy, and kind. And right then, in that season of our lives, we were checking all three boxes. Sometimes we won't be checking all three. Sometimes it will be hard to check any boxes at all. I told her we didn't need to measure in quantity and that quality was more important.

Having a few good friends who really know you and love you is better than trying to be everything to everyone.

Some boys won't like you back, and it will hurt, but you'll be okay. You can always love yourself and pay attention to yourself.

There's more to life than free drinks; just trust me on this one.

The folks you want to be spending time with will love you, first and foremost, and they'll understand that your body is a vehicle for that bright and sparkly soul of yours. Your size will fluctuate, and as long as you're happy and you feel good, ultimately nothing else matters.

Little Sydney had a moment, looking myself up and down.

Well done, sis. Way to take care of us.

As I got closer to the water, I considered turning around and asking Barry to join me, but I was feeling shy and didn't want to bother him while he finished setting up the tent. So I found myself a spot with the rock formation and ocean in the background, shoved the GoPro into the sand, and turned on the camera to take some pictures of myself.

The first one I took was perfect.

Great, I thought, *now I won't get caught being a total weirdo over here!*

After my solo photo shoot and journal time, we made dinner and went on an expedition.

Our mission: acquire bison chips. And by chips, I mean poop. Bison poop. We were looking for piles of bison poop. We read that it makes

Feeling like a total babe on the beach in Little Harbor.

a great fuel source for a fire, so we took a lap around the campground and picked up dried piles of bison poop. It sounds gross, but really it's just digested grass; there isn't much else to it. When we got back to the campsite, there were some dried-out palm fronds on the ground beneath the tree near our tent. Barry started working on the fire as I got the water boiling on the camp stove for our dessert: raspberry chocolate crumble. Sounds fancy, but it's not really. It's a mix of dehydrated raspberry puree plus a packet of crushed-up chocolate cookies to mimic an Oreo crust. We'd had it on our first trip, and I was stoked to have something sweet for my birthday. That was one of the first desserts I'd had since I was diagnosed with diabetes, and I was excited for the occasion.

As the water came to a boil, Barry started shouting about the fire he started. I looked around and saw the lighter still on the table. Wait a minute. How did he do that?

He had dug deep beneath the surface ash and found some still kinda-hot embers from a fire the night before. I thought it was pure magic. The fire burned pretty hot through the smaller timber, and the logs we found at our campsite lit quickly. As the sunset faded and the stars came out, Barry started placing the bison chips around the embers. As they caught fire, they went straight to smoldering. It smelled like mescal—ashy, but also floral and vegetal.

We sat by the fire, passing a bag of raspberry chocolate crumble back and forth between us. Barry turned on his headlamp to grab another palm frond, and as he panned the area around our campsite, we saw a bunch of animal eyes. Squirrels, scampering away. A deer and her baby. A couple of Catalina Island foxes—a species endemic to the island, found nowhere else in the world. It was wild. We were only under the tarp, so we made sure we put everything that wasn't a pillow, sleeping pad, or sleeping bag in the fox box. We didn't want any visitors in the tent.

The next day was our day off, and I had big plans. It was overcast, and that side of the island was a bit chilly, so we bundled up, took our time making breakfast, and walked over to our campsite from the first trip.

They very well could have changed the campground layout between 2016 and our second trip, but once we got up there, I looked at the tree we'd slept under on the night of the rainstorm and over across the road to where the porta-potties were. It didn't seem that far. I could barely walk on that trip and every step took the effort of ten with my cinder-block feet, but I couldn't help but giggle to myself.

We joked about the bison prints looking like Jurassic Park, my Lady Gaga–style muddy hiking shoes and rain gear ensemble, and the poor trail conditions.

As we walked down to Whale's Tail Rock, I knew which photos I wanted. I wanted Outdoor Goddess Standing on a Rock Looking at the Ocean, and this was the place to do it. I looked at what I was wearing:

Sydney the Outdoor Fashion Icon on Whale's Tail Rock between Shark Harbor and Little Harbor.

trail runners, my green socks I'd gotten in memory of Adam, black trekking tights, a neon-blue long sleeve, a purple vest, and a gray beanie. It was quite the look, especially for the first week of June on an island.

I didn't care. I rocked that little photo shoot. Mismatched clothes and all. We spent the rest of the day taking pictures at Shark Harbor, watching the waves, exploring more of the rock formations, and sitting on the beach near our campsite.

As the sun started to set, I pulled out my notebook and reread my entry from my birthday.

Maybe I'm realizing that I was whole when I got here and I'll be whole when I leave, and I don't NEED this to be some big thing, because by the very nature of it happening, it IS a big thing.

I sat there in awe of the clarity I had found. Hiking my feelings, indeed. I grinned to myself. I read that part over and over, really trying to wrap my head around what wholeness felt like in that moment. So far I'd had some high highs and was moving a lot of old energy through my body. Something was clearly happening.

Is this island magic? Did I die on the way here and is this heaven?

TRAIL OF LIFE

When I think back on my mindset around my weight and body image, I divide it into two timelines and categories. Prior to that dressing room before the first hike, every choice I made in the name of health was rooted in vanity, aka my fear of being fat. After that dressing-room moment, every choice I made was rooted in love for myself.

So if I can make the recommendation again, whenever you can, choose love over fear.

We hear the following phrases often, especially in spaces and communities that are intending to promote wellness and healing:

The choice is yours.

Happiness is a choice, so just choose happiness.

Everything is a choice.

All of that is true, but the reason it feels so disingenuous, the reason it feels so floaty and lofty and unattainable, is that short phrases make better slogans. They're easier to understand, and they don't require much critical thinking. When we stop the conversation with a declaration instead of digging deeper, we sell ourselves short. Without the nuance, there's no acknowledgment that we aren't all born on the same foundation from which to make choices. We don't hold space for different family dynamics, financial situations, community support (or lack thereof), and we lack understanding of other folks' lived experiences.

That's why talking about this is so damn important. If we keep our stories to ourselves, we rob humanity of the opportunity to understand one another. Owning what we've been through, at least with ourselves, is the first step to feeling comfortable talking about it. The weight of conversations about weight is heavy, and unpacking it is exhausting, but we've got to do the work if we want to be truly free from the power it has over us. The second we let someone else in, the second we pass some of our heavy load to another person who is willing and able to help us carry it, we get one step closer to freedom.

If you're anything like me and have been holding off on living your life until you reach a certain weight, I have some news to share. It's not worth the wait. Please, for the love of everything holy, righteous, and wonderful, go live your life right now. Don't wait another second to reach some arbitrary standard of beauty to feel worthy. You are whole and complete and wonderful exactly as you are right now. And if that makes you cringe and roll your eyes, I've been there too. It's hard to believe that we're worthy and awesome when the entire world doesn't reflect that back to us.

I also want to say there is absolutely nothing wrong with wanting to be healthy. There is absolutely nothing wrong with taking action to improve your day-to-day life. If weight loss is a by-product of the efforts you're making for your mental, physical, and spiritual health, then high five for you. But if I've learned anything since my diagnosis and subsequent weight loss, it's that the world keeps spinning and changing and doing whatever it wants to do, regardless of what your body looks like and how much you weigh.

When I was first getting into backpacking, I wore the biggest sizes sold at REI. They did not carry larger than a size sixteen pants or an XL shirt. It wasn't until after I started losing weight that they started selling larger sizes. When I needed bigger sizes, I couldn't find any of them. Around the same time I started to accept my body and started losing weight as a side effect of my diabetes management protocol, there was a massive influx of conversations online, in the media, and in my communities about body positivity. In the months that followed my first hike on the TCT, REI included plus-size women in their advertising for the first time ever.

I had whiplash. When I was bigger, I didn't see myself represented in advertising for outdoor equipment or experiences, and I had to squeeze into the sizes they had. After I started losing weight, I saw bodies that looked like mine used to in ads for the activities I was growing to love. Obviously I was stoked that the sizes had expanded so hopefully other women wouldn't feel like me, but I was also pissed off. I was pissed that I had internalized so much messaging and had been making significant decisions about my life and the experiences I was having based on the size of my body. I was pissed that when I needed bigger sizes I couldn't get them. Pissed that when I was finally losing weight it was okay to be bigger. Pissed that this was impacting me as deeply as it was. Pissed at my own internalized misogyny and fatphobia.

I hate to break it to you, but all of the prizes that are promised when we reach that illusive perfect size are a load of bullshit, and they don't change anything about how awesome you are, right here, right now, exactly as you are. Turns out, upon reaching your goal weight, a bartender doesn't come busting through your door offering free drinks. Your middle school crush doesn't show up with flowers professing his love for you. You don't get a parade.

At the end of the day, this part of my journey could be summarized by a phrase I've been utilizing as a mantra to counter the torture we put ourselves through every year as summer approaches: If you have a body and you're wearing a bikini, congratulations, you have a bikini body!

MINDFUL MILES

Alright, folks, let's have a real talk about weight loss. Shedding those pounds might give you a temporary confidence boost, but let me tell you, it doesn't solve all of life's problems. Happiness and fulfillment aren't found in a number on a scale. True joy comes from embracing your worth beyond your appearance—cultivating meaningful relationships, pursuing passions, and nourishing your mind, body, and soul. So, let's shift our focus away from the pursuit of a perfect figure and start prioritizing self-love, acceptance, and holistic well-being.

- What have you been denying yourself while you wait until you have a perfect body? Love? Sex? Food? New hobbies? Social interactions?

- What are some choices you've made from a place of fear? How did those choices work out for you?

- What are some choices you've made from a place of love? How did *those* choices work out for you?

NEXT STEPS

Ready to take this practice up a notch? It's time to get rid of the clothing that doesn't fit you. We are under no obligation to surround ourselves with reminders of our failure to be perfect, because perfection is a construct, not reality. If you're anything like me before I downsized my wardrobe dramatically following the hike in 2018, you probably have a section of your closet or a special drawer that contains the *someday clothes*: the clothes that you hang on to in hopes that they'll fit again someday.

Bodies change; we know this. So why do we hold ourselves hostage by hanging on to pieces of fabric that no longer serve a purpose on the bodies we live in today? Perhaps it's nostalgia. I've held on to the skydiving jumpsuit I wore when I got married in the way a lot of women save their wedding dresses. Perhaps we've internalized a belief that we can shame ourselves into being smaller, and if we're persistent enough, someday we'll hate ourselves enough to take dramatic and unhealthy actions to reduce the weight we carry every day. Or maybe you've been so busy with life that you just haven't made time to do a little closet cleanup.

If you've never downsized your material belongings before, this might feel like a personal attack. After a lifetime of being marketed to by every brand out there looking to help you part ways with your money, and working extra hard to earn what you spend, it can be incredibly difficult to wrap your head around having less in a society that teaches us to always be striving for more. If you worked really hard and saved money for a long time to purchase something that no longer fits, you could be navigating body image issues that are compounded by worthiness challenges and a money mindset: *Look at how out of control I am! These clothes no longer fit, which just goes to show that I can't have nice things!*

Do what you need to do to feel comfortable with letting go of the clothes that no longer fit you. Think about the memories you created in those pieces. Think of how you felt when you were buying them. Hold space for the feelings of inadequacy that may surface as you start separating those items out of your rotation.

When it feels overwhelming, remind yourself of the facts. Bodies change for a whole multitude of reasons. And if you're reading this, you survived all of that. Taking some clothes out of your closet may feel like a huge endeavor for all the reasons listed and whatever other reasons are revealed as you go through the process, but if you can make it through everything life has dealt you thus far, you can do this too.

And if you get to your closet and it feels like a full-body "Hell no" to go through this practice, give yourself some grace. You don't have to do everything all at once. You can start with one piece, go through the process of removing it from your rotation, and pick this up again another day.

CHAPTER 14

EMBRACE YOUR STINK

Reclaiming Your Body

I woke up in the cold the next morning and made tea to help warm myself up. After the sweaty cruise from the airport into Little Harbor, I was okay with a breeze and some clouds. As we packed up to head over to Two Harbors, I gave myself a wet-wipe shower and put on more deodorant.

I went to the trash can to toss the wipes and I still had the deodorant in my hand. I tossed the wipes and turned back toward our campsite. I took a few steps and stopped, looked back at the trash can, then back at the campsite, then at the deodorant in my hand.

Did I need to bring deodorant on a backpacking trip? Turns out it's a waste of space and pack weight, because after four days on a trail without a shower, you're going to start to smell. That's just how it goes. Even with my dip in the ocean on my birthday, I was still pretty ripe, thus the wipe down.

I started to walk back toward the trash can. I lifted the lid, then put it down.

The deodorant wasn't physically heavy. I had saved the end of my last tube of deodorant for the trip so I didn't have to bring a full tube, so it didn't add much weight to my backpack. But emotionally? *Woooo* lord, the deodorant felt like an anvil in my hand. It was the same brand I tested on the first TCT hike, a product of the beauty startup I eventually became CMO of for those ninety-five glorious days. The deodorant was loaded with emotional baggage. It was the first product I'd tried that Brenda made. When the all-natural deodorant kept me from smelling disgusting all the way across the trail the first time, I officially became a believer in the products she was making. When I got home from that first hike, I raved about the deodorant. I knew that personal care products were typically loaded with chemicals and I wanted to know more. If the deodorant was so great, what was the skin-care line all about? I wanted to know everything. I'd had no idea back then that I'd ever work with her at that company, that I'd be CMO at that company, or that I'd quit after ninety-five days. I certainly didn't know that I'd be on the TCT two weeks after leaving the company, with nothing else in my way and no responsibilities other than safely hiking across the island.

On my first trip, I identified that I had been sold a bag of shit by the beauty-industrial complex. I had spent my whole life trying to fit into a box, and on the trail the first time we attempted the hike, I'd found love for a body I didn't recognize. I had never felt that way about myself. Standing at the trash can with a tube of deodorant in my hand, the metaphors were almost too much to bear.

I thought about what that tube of deodorant represented to me on the trip: the end of a relationship. Beyond that, the deodorant simply no longer worked for me. I don't know if the formulation changed or if it was a rushed batch during the big orders, but I smelled to high heaven at home, let alone after four days and nearly twenty miles on the trail.

As if on cue, Barry came cruising past with a wisdom drive-by. "Hey, ditch the deodorant, embrace your stink," he said, cool as a cucumber.

I picked up the lid and chucked the tube into the trash. I immediately felt lighter, like I did in the dressing room the first time, and after all the crying about my friends who had passed. Was the trash can a portal? Was the deodorant actually weighing me down spiritually and emotionally? Or was it another opportunity to check in with myself and examine some of the items in my trauma pack?

I raised my arm to smell my pits. *What died in here?*

"Embrace my stink?" I scoffed. "But I'm so ripe!"

Then I thought about it. *The last time I hiked this trail, I focused on breaking down the myths I bought into about beauty standards. On this trip, I'm chucking this deodorant in the trash. I don't need any of it. I'm going to embrace my stink!*

We all have a scent. Mine was unpleasant at that moment, but our scent is what makes us us. What else made me me? What are the things that people have said are bad or wrong or gross about my body that I have been trying to fix for years that I just physically cannot fix?

I looked at my thumbs.

I have brachydactyly type D, better known as *clubbed thumbs,* or as my sister liked to tease me, *toe thumbs.* I didn't know anything was wrong with my thumbs until my sister jeered at me one day after school, "You know boys don't like girls with toe thumbs."

Sick burn.

For the rest of my adolescence, well into the seventh or eighth grade, I'd walked around with my thumbs tucked into my palm, forming a fist to hide them. Kids being kids, sisters being the worst to each other, was it true? Probably not. Did I know that? Of course not. So I'd hid my thumbs, hoping and praying that would maybe give me a shot in hell at meeting a boy and making friends.

I looked at my thumbs as I went back to the picnic table to grab my gear and carry on to Two Harbors. I knew what was coming: We had a big climb out of the campground and then one of the huge sections with no switchbacks. It was going to be a brutal morning, but at least it wasn't sunny. The clouds would help us again today.

As we started hiking, I got a bit indignant about the thumb thing.

My thumbs are adorable. When I give a thumbs up, it may be small and mighty, but there's no question that these are thumbs and they are up. I found a boy who likes me. Wait. Has Barry seen my thumbs?

"Babe! Have you seen my thumbs?" I shouted down to Barry.

I was leading the way then, and I was Betty-goating (lady version of being a billy goat) up the sucker. He couldn't hear me. I didn't want to repeat it, so I just flashed him a thumbs-up.

He flashed one back.

I started crying.

I paused, got a sip of water, and took off my hat to wipe my forehead. I contemplated getting my cold towel out, but I knew we were climbing to one of the most gorgeous views on the hike, and the wind was already picking up. I let my hair blow around in the breeze, cooling my head down. As I ran my fingers through my hair to pull it back into a ponytail, my fingernail got snagged on a tangle.

I had a visceral reaction to the tangle and paused.

Where did that come from?

It reminded me of when I'd gotten scolded for not straightening my hair for work.

It was the summer of 2010. I had just started skydiving and I was working at a prestigious PR firm in downtown Chicago. If you've seen *The Devil Wears Prada*, it was like that, fashionwise. The folks that worked there weren't nearly as vicious as the characters in the movie, but sometimes the halls felt like a fashion

Climbing straight up on our way out of Little Harbor, embracing my stink.

runway. Coming from a suburb of Kansas City, I had some catching up to do on all fronts related to business casual and corporate-appropriate makeup and hairstyles.

If you know me today, you know I wear my hair in its natural state. But prior to that section of the trail I had been beholden to a straightener for the better part of two decades. When I was working at the agency, the expectation was to look client-ready at all times. I was working in the Chicago office, which was one of the largest offices for the agency, and a lot of our clients were based in Chicago. You never knew who was in the building.

When I'd first started working there, I was making $10 per hour as an intern. When I got hired full-time I started earning $30K per year. Moving to a city where I didn't know anyone landed me in a studio apartment by myself. Add in a monthly bus pass, paying back student loans, car insurance, groceries, and there wasn't much left at the end of the month. Besides, fashion had never been my priority.

I was a cheerleader for most of my school years and wore our uniforms to school on game days, so I didn't need a lot of clothes. When I went to KU, I was on the rowing team and we had team gear that I wore to class most days, since we usually had both weights and conditioning sessions and actual rowing practice. Didn't need a lot of clothes for college either.

So it being my first job that wasn't in a restaurant, and not having a ton of money, I'd skirted the line of business casual and straight-up casual more often than not.

When Barry and I started dating, I wanted to spend as much time at the drop zone—another name for a skydiving center—as I could. I would drive to the office on Friday morning and pay to park in a lot like one of the senior executives did, all so I could get out to the drop zone on Friday after work. I rarely made it in time to get a jump in before sunset, but I didn't care; I just wanted to hang out with Barry around the bonfire after he got done working.

I'd spend all day Saturday and Sunday at the drop zone, jumping out of planes, helping where needed, chatting with Barry between jumps. I'd spend Sunday night at Barry's and then wake up Monday morning, shower and get ready, then drive into the office, park at the garage, and go to work.

When I started pulling these longer weekends, I'd bring a bag with a change of clothes for work on Monday, my straightener, and my makeup.

The drop zone was the first place I'd found since moving to Illinois where I felt like I could be me, fully expressed. I could wear my comfy athletic clothes and not be judged. I could shower and let my hair dry naturally, letting my waves and curls do what they do. I didn't wear makeup when I was jumping out of planes. I was just me. And it was glorious.

Until one weekend I forgot my bag and didn't realize it until Monday morning. I'd gone out to my car to grab my shower stuff and it wasn't there. No clothes. No straightener.

Damn it.

Fortunately both of Barry's roommates were quite social with the female skydiving students and licensed jumpers, so I'd been able to find some shampoo and conditioner in the bathroom. My hair wouldn't be straight, but I could wear it wavy and pull it back a bit to class it up. I could pull it off. I had the outfit I wore Friday. Fortunately I'd changed for the bonfire, so it didn't smell of campfire and it was still clean. But Fridays were definitely super casual, and the outfit I'd worn the previous Friday was very casual. It was all I'd had, and I'd rather have been on time and not totally client-ready than go all the way back to my apartment before work and end up being super late.

I'd gotten ready as best I could, kissed Barry goodbye, and went to the office.

I was early; good.

Our office was in an old medical building, and everyone except interns had their own office with a door.

I think I'm going to be okay, I thought as I'd closed my door behind me.

I sat down, started up my computer, and checked my calendar. All clear until ten.

Great. I can actually get some work done this morning.

Then I'd gotten a new email. A note from a colleague asking me to come by her office. The woman was my assigned mentor, someone I was paired with by HR when I'd made the transition from intern to full-time employee. Her role was to help me stay on track, producing quality work, abiding by company policy, all of that.

Shit shit shit shit shit. She saw me. I'm in trouble.

I'd walked to her office, head hung in shame like a kid on the way to the principal's office.

I knocked twice. She motioned for me to come in. I sat down as she finished what she was typing.

She looked me up and down.

Yep, here it comes.

She wouldn't stop looking at my hair. "So, good morning. How was your weekend?"

Jesus, lady, let's get on with it already.

"It was great. I spent all weekend at the drop zone, which, by the way—"

She cut me off. "We have clients in the building today."

Ah, agency-speak for "What the hell are you wearing and why are you making me have this conversation with you?"

"I know, I'm so sorry, it won't happen again."

"It just, well, when you aren't client-ready it looks unprofessional. We don't want to look unprofessional or unreliable."

"No, of course not. Again, I'm super sorry."

She dismissed me and I went back to my office.

Okay, got it. If I want to stay gainfully employed this cannot happen again. God, I hope she doesn't tell my boss. I hope this doesn't turn into an Office Space *situation, where people keep coming up to me asking if I knew we have clients in the building.*

Back on the trail, I finished pulling my hair back, put my hat back on, and continued hiking.

I envisioned myself as my own Flavor Flav, the hype man from Public Enemy back in the day. I was hyping myself all the way up. It worked with the thumbs thing; I thought I'd give it a go with the hair.

Nah, girl, your hair is siiiiick. So many folks would spend good money to get texture like that. People buy products, get treatments, use devices to get hair like yours. And what, you woke up like that? Your hair is gorgeous, and honestly, your hair has nothing to do with whether or not you're professional or reliable. If anyone ever says that to you again, you don't need that negativity in your life, professionally or personally.

Next I heard my uncle Mike's voice.

Don't you dare cover up those tattoos, Sydney.

While I have several tattoos, I've always covered them up. Paddleboarding helped me get over my irrational fear of people killing themselves at the sight of my exposed skin, but as far as my clothing choices were concerned, I was still hiding my arms and midsection. I thought about all the times I had covered up, making myself unnecessarily uncomfortable. Covering up because I wasn't confident in my own skin and didn't want to be seen. I thought of all the invitations and opportunities I'd turned down because I didn't want people to see me like that in my bigger body.

Standing on the Amtrak platform at Union Station in LA. July. Temperatures hovering around 95 degrees Fahrenheit. Trains throwing heat. Probably more than 120 degrees waiting for the train doors to open. Sweat dripping down my back. On my way back to San Diego after spending three days in LA at the NBC offices. What am I wearing? A long-sleeve shirt, black pants, ballet flats. Just trying to blend in.

I'd almost passed out that day while I was waiting for the train. I'd chosen to be uncomfortably hot so I could be comfortably invisible in public. As long as I wasn't being seen, life was good.

Thank goddess Barry recommended paddleboarding. That's done wonders for my confidence in my body.

I had lived in Southern California for seven years, and it wasn't until the summer of 2017 that I'd felt comfortable spending time in a swimsuit on the water. How many more memories could I have made? I hadn't gone to my high school reunion. I'd passed on opportunities that required nicer clothes because I didn't really have any.

I will never turn down another opportunity because I don't think I have time to lose weight before the event or because I don't feel fashionable enough.

As we neared the top, I turned into my own hype man again.

Listen, your tattoos are sick. You paid good money for that art and you know you love them; don't hide them anymore. Let people see what you've got!

It hit me. Three of my five tattoos were skydiving related, or I'd gotten them at a skydiving event. The other two were memorial pieces. Yes, the art was great. Yes, I wished my arms were more toned, but that wasn't only about my tattoos themselves or my discomfort in my body. Every tattoo I have starts a conversation. And until right then, on the side of that mountain, I hadn't been ready to share the stories that correspond with each tattoo because the memories themselves were too painful.

I went through my tattoos in order, reclaiming the stories of how and why I got them and why they were significant—a wrist tattoo the summer I'd started skydiving, "Total Freedom" on my foot, a half sleeve representing my love of the water and the sky, and another half sleeve as a memorial for my grandmother.

The last tattoo I had done was a memorial for Adam.

I went back to Outer Limits Tattoo (the shop owned by the artist who did the tattoo for my grandmother) with Adam's mom and sister in tow. They were in town for his memorial skydive, which I was coordinating as a function of Planet Green Socks.

At the visitation following Adam's death, his mom and sister had read a poem called "The Dash" by Linda Ellis. It talks about how on our tombstone there's the day we were born and the day we die, and in between—that dash—is the life we live on this planet. The poem goes on to ask readers to reflect on how they live their dash. It was the perfect poem for Adam's funeral. He was only twenty-three when he died, but he lived a big life. He lived his dash. So all three of us were going to get "Live Your Dash" tattooed on our forearms, with some kind of illustration that reminded us of Adam.

Next to the words "Live Your Dash" I wanted a feather to represent Adam's eternal flight. He earned his wings now. His mom chose a couple of elements from Adam's full-sleeve tattoo—a timer filled with sand and a pair of dice. His sister got a compass, a reminder of his love of travel and her desire to keep traveling in his memory.

Turns out if you want to get through a sucktastic portion of a hike, reclaiming parts of your body is the way to do it without being totally consumed by the difficulty. By the time I was done reminiscing about tattoos I was at the top of the peak. Despite the challenge, I felt incredible. I was out of breath, sweating like it was a hundred degrees outside, and that process on the way up released some serious weight for me.

I took off my shirt. I was making up for lost time.

Sydney Williams doesn't wear shirts anymore.

I asked Barry to take pictures of me on top of the peak. I put my hands on my hips like a superhero and took a few deep breaths, taking in the view on top of that peak, standing in my power for the first time. I had just reclaimed parts of my body that people had told me I should

Power posing on a cliff is all the rage. Thank you for coming to my TED Talk.

fix. I'd gained an appreciation for my body on the first hike across the island, but the second hike was something completely different.

I took off my hat and walked to the edge of the cliff. I threw my arms up with glee, thanking the island for carrying the weight of the memories I was recounting.

The wind picked up again, and I let my hair down. It was tangled and matted after four days on the trail with no shower, and some of the natural texture was coming back. The wind whipped around my body, cooling me down rapidly on top of the peak. I scanned the surrounding area, observing the dramatic cliffs dropping into the ocean, looking back to where we'd come from, looking ahead to what was still in store for us on the upcoming section of trail.

This is new territory, I thought. *Geographically, everything after Two Harbors is new to us. Physically, I've never hiked this far in so many days. What will I feel like tomorrow? The day after that? What is Parsons going to be like? What about the route to get there? Emotionally, this is also new territory. I'm working through some serious stuff so far on this trail, and while there has been a significant amount of crying, none of this is scary. None of this makes me sad. With each step I feel more and more like myself. With each step I feel like I'm getting closer to the woman I have always known I could be.*

Confident that Barry got the shot, I turned around, made a beeline for my shirt, and got dressed again. It was chilly up on the cliff, and I was really looking forward to getting into Two Harbors and grabbing a Buffalo Milk.

TRAIL OF LIFE

On the first hike along the TCT, I said that one of the takeaways was "I love my body," and in those moments, it really felt like I did. But after going up the mountain and going through the process of reclaiming my shine, I realized that what I'd felt back in 2016 was *neutrality* around my body. I didn't hate it anymore; I had started to accept it for what it was without judgment. Standing on the top of the mountain between Little Harbor and Two Harbors, I felt whole, complete, connected. I had been so disgusted by my body for so long, and going through this process of embracing my stink helped me reestablish my mind-body connection.

As I marched up one of the ridgelines between Little Harbor and Two Harbors, I was pulling out more heavy items from my trauma pack— things people had said I should change about my body that I physically can't or was tired of trying to fix. I reclaimed my thumbs, my hair, and my tattoos. When I got done exploring that trauma, I replaced it with the positive things I said to myself, lightening the backpack once again. And in return, at the top, I felt powerful in my body for the first time.

You are a miracle. Think about it. What are the odds that your parents would meet out of the billions of people on this planet? What are the odds that they'd decide to bring you into this world, whether it was planned, a surprise, or if you were adopted or raised in a foster home?

What are the chances that you would survive childbirth? What are the chances that you'd make it here, today, to be reading these words?

Take a deep breath. Regardless of what *divine* means to you, you are a miracle from the divine. Whether you practice a certain religion, hold faith in the stars, planets, and the universe at large, or have some other belief system that connects you to something bigger than yourself, you're here, and that's pretty damn special.

The things that have happened to you may shape your character, belief systems, and the way you see yourself and the way you carry yourself, but the things that have happened to you do not have to define you. We are under no obligation to wear our trauma as an identity, and if you've been carrying these stories and holding on to them because the pain is all you know, it might feel impossible to see yourself as anything other than the list of things you've endured. I want to be sure I'm clear here: It is entirely possible to honor and have deep respect for what we (and our ancestors) have been through *and* define ourselves in other ways. Two things can be true at once.

The way your mind works, the way your body works, and the way your spirit shines are unique to you. Do you believe that?

When you start to revisit the old memories, the old behaviors, and the old ways of thinking, it can be painful. But armed with enough compassion you can remind yourself that you didn't know what you didn't know. Repeat after me: "I didn't know what I didn't know."

The awareness and the action are the work, and that cannot be done without dousing yourself in compassion and forgiveness. There are so many factors that play into how we see ourselves: our parents, our immediate family, our extended family, the media we consume, our teachers, friends, work colleagues. For the first seven to twelve years we are on this planet, we are sponges, absorbing the education provided, verbal cues, body language, and happenings around us. We are told who we are, what we are like.

This is a chance to reclaim the stories you've been telling yourself. This is a chance to rewrite the ending. If you don't like the way your story is playing out, remember that you are the author, and how this story ends is your choice. Do you want to be your own hero, or do you want to keep believing the lies you've been feeding yourself? The choice is yours.

MINDFUL MILES

Are you ready to reclaim your body and release the weight of society's expectations and judgments? Shift your focus from external ideals to inner strength and self-care. Nourish yourself with wholesome foods, move your body in ways that feel joyful, and cultivate a loving relationship with every inch of your being. Celebrate the unique curves, scars, and features that make you beautifully you. Remember, your body is your sanctuary, and it's time to honor and cherish it. You deserve to know, love, and respect your body inside and out.

- Are there parts of your body that cause you anxiety or shame? Are there parts of your body you'd like to reclaim? What is one thing you could do to build a loving relationship with those parts of your body?

- What are things about your body that people (or the media you consume) have told you are bad or wrong that you've been trying to fix?

- Have you thanked your body for how it works for you today? This week? This month? The past year? Even if it feels scary, unsafe, or foreign to think of our bodies in this way, if you're reading this, you're alive. Start there.

NEXT STEPS

Pay attention to your energy over the next week or so. Where do you give your attention? Do you want to keep doing that? Nothing says you have to keep doing what you're doing. Don't be afraid to switch it up.

- If you find yourself frustrated, I encourage you to ask yourself, "Is this mine?"

- If you get triggered and have a reaction that feels out of your control, ask yourself, "Is this mine?"

- If you look at parts of your body with anything less than loving affection and appreciation, ask yourself, "Is this mine?"

- If you are feeling down, like your spirit has been crushed, ask yourself why. When you arrive at the answer to that question, ask yourself, "Is this mine?"

CHAPTER 15

BE YOUR OWN BEST FRIEND

Unpacking Your Negative Thoughts

As we continued hiking to Two Harbors, I was having a hard time staying present and enjoying the moment. My mind kept wandering to the things I didn't know about the trail. I had read the maps and done my research, but my personal experience on the trail ended at Two Harbors, and I didn't have any intel about the section between Two Harbors and Parsons Landing. The map we had with us showed elevation gain like that first day from Avalon to Black Jack, but it looked like it was just one big mountain versus up and down five peaks.

If we can find someone who's already hiked this section, that would be great.

As we got closer to town, Barry and I started chatting feverishly about the burgers we'd had last time we were in Two Harbors.

"Were they really that good?" I asked. "I mean, we hiked twenty-some miles to get those burgers. Do you think they're really the best burgers we've ever had or were they just so good because they weren't food in a bag?"

"Oh, I think they're that good. It was freaking Kobe beef, for crying out loud. Those are happy cows!" Barry replied.

Everything about that stretch of trail felt like a trip down memory lane.

"This is where we had to wander through the fields because the road was so muddy!" Barry called out.

"This is where we got turned around and that nice couple asked us if we needed help!" I shouted as we made our way into town.

We made a beeline for the office on the dock where we would check in. I knew where the campground was, and while I was sore, I wasn't completely incapable of making it another mile uphill. We checked in, got our key for our locker at Parsons the next day, and made our way up to the campsite.

We wandered through a group camp, a private campsite, and then onto the main campground. We were right by our own little cove. As we rolled up, the folks who were at the spot the night before were packing up. They had miniature cans of Diet Dr Pepper and a couple bottles of Martinelli's Apple Juice—the good stuff.

"Do you guys want any of this?" one of them asked.

"Sure! Thanks!" we said, scooping up the cans and bottles.

We set up camp, our tarp and trekking poles serving as a makeshift tent again. We tucked our gear away in the tent and made our way down to the restaurant.

It was burger time.

Now that it was summer, the outdoor patio was open, so we snagged a table on the beach and waited for the server. I scanned the menu, as if I would order anything other than the burger. When the server came, we were more than ready.

"I'll have the Harbor Reef burger, onion rings, and a Buffalo Milk, please," I said.

The server looked at Barry.

"I'll have the exact same thing, thanks!"

We watched the waves roll in, watched hikers find their way to the office on the dock and then up to the campground. Our drinks arrived,

Making up for the diabetes documentary photo shoot by channeling my inner tiger on Catalina Island.

and we toasted to how far we had come, both literally across the island and in the grander sense—together as a couple, me managing diabetes and all of the changes along the way.

Shortly thereafter our burgers arrived. I could smell them before I could see our server.

That first bite was just as magical as it was on the last trip. Eye roll inducing. I cannot confirm or deny, but there may have been a slight moan.

As much as I would have loved to savor every single bite, that didn't happen. I was famished. We inhaled the burgers and rings, agreeing that the burger was even better than we remembered it being, and ordered another Buffalo Milk for dessert. After I ordered, I paused and started doing the math around calories and blood sugar, considering if I could really afford to have a second Buffalo Milk.

I had just hiked twenty-six miles across the trail. My blood sugar was spectacular so far. Historically, my relationship with food had been so chaotic, but diabetes gave me permission to finally take control of my life, no excuses. I didn't want the Buffalo Milk to be the thing that made me slide back to more than two hundred pounds with blood sugar through the roof.

Get it together, Sydney. Listen to your body. If you want another Buffalo Milk, have one, but don't beat yourself up about it. You're doing great.

I snapped out of my shame spiral. Damn straight I could make healthy choices. And damn straight I had the discipline and desire to keep diabetes at bay. End of story.

I enjoyed a second Buffalo Milk and then we walked back to the campsite. We met a couple along the way who were doing the trail in reverse.

Ask and the universe provides, I thought.

The couple had just completed the loop out to Parsons and was settling into Two Harbors today before continuing on toward Little Harbor tomorrow.

I asked them what the route to Parsons Landing was like and they confirmed my understanding.

There were two routes out to the last campground. If you wanted to follow the trail in sequential order, then the route out of Two Harbors was challenging. Yes, it was similar to the first day on-trail. Yes, that elevation gain was done in one fell swoop. No, there weren't many switchbacks. It was all uphill, all day. And then of course, what goes up must come down. The descent into Parsons Landing was very steep, and the terrain was that loose gravelly stuff, so have your poles ready, watch your step, take your time, and hike your own hike. The return route out of Parsons Landing back to Two Harbors, the section they had just completed, was a nice, flat dirt road that hugs the coastline. It was like your victory lap to end the trip: no real elevation gains to worry about, just gorgeous views of all the little coves along the way.

I thanked them for the intel, and they split off to go to their campsite. Barry asked me which way I wanted to go in the morning.

Knowing I can do hard things, one of the lessons I learned on the first trip, I wanted to go the hard way. Get it over with. If we had enough energy to keep going out to Starlight Beach, we could do that too.

When we got back to the campsite I busted out my little notebook. The hike from Little Harbor was pretty powerful and I wanted to remember what I had experienced.

We called it an early night and fell asleep to the sound of waves lapping at the rocks below our campsite. When I woke up, Barry said he wanted to get breakfast in town, so we packed up and headed to the restaurant. I ordered a bagel with smoked salmon and Barry got a breakfast sandwich. We sat down outside and enjoyed our breakfast as the rest of the hikers started to wake up. As we finished, we saw another couple donning big backpacks heading toward the start of the loop to Parsons. Following suit, we packed up and made our way back to the trail.

As we climbed out of the harbor toward the ridgeline, I heard a voice pop into my head. *When shit gets hard, you run.*

I had been hearing that off and on throughout the hike and in the weeks preceding it. I was hoping I could just hike it out, but like I said earlier, I can't bypass the talking-it-out part. So up the mountain I talked it out. With myself.

When shit gets hard, you run. The first time I heard it, it sounded like my voice in my head. As if I were saying it to myself.

Thinking back to when I was in the dressing room the first time, I wondered if I would ever talk to myself like that. No, I wouldn't. I thought back to some of the prior meditations I had exercised about releasing people, situations, behaviors, and habits that no longer served me.

What would it feel like to let that go? I wondered.

As I kept hiking up to one of the highest points on the island, I imagined weight being lifted off my shoulders as I released the power I gave that phrase. I felt lighter and my pace quickened.

After a while it came back into my head. *When shit gets hard, you run.*

That time it didn't sound like my inner voice. It sounded like my former business partner. I could see the way her head would move when she said that to my face. The flash of disgust in her eyes, as if I were a problem to be fixed when I had a panic attack in her living room. I imagined more weight being lifted, letting go of that phrase again. I didn't feel lighter. It felt like I was stuck in that emotion, that loop, like it was a CD and it was skipping on that one phrase. Recalling how I felt at the top of one of the peaks yesterday after being my own hype man up that tough climb on the ridgeline, I thought about how I might pump myself up again. I also thought back to that dressing room, when I was talking to myself like I would speak to my best friend. I tried looking at it from that angle. What would Kat tell me if she were trying to pump me up in that situation?

Okay, Sydney. Listen, you've jumped out of an airplane nearly 700 times. That's hard. And you've moved all over this country for love and work. Find a thing, uproot your life, land somewhere else. Multiple times. Even if you like doing it, transplanting again and again is a lot. I'd say that's hard.

Ooh, and you're coming up on thirty miles hiked across this island. That's hard, too!

I stopped to catch my breath. I felt lighter and I was crying. I was so happy and feeling so floaty I didn't even realize I was crying.

I couldn't make sense of it. We were on one of the steepest parts of the island, and I was cruising. Where was the energy coming from? I kept hiking, feeling more energized than I had since we first got on the trail five days ago. I realized that the last time I had done this I didn't know that I could, so with every step I was proving myself wrong. I knew I could do it, and with every step I was proving myself right.

We had a considerable distance to cover so we kept moving, and as we did, more thoughts bubbled up to the surface. More one-liners that had stuck with me and become my internal soundtrack, my negative self-talk, ready to take me down the second I felt too confident.

Watch out for her wrath. She's violent.

Hmm, I didn't like that.

I imagined what it would feel like to let that go, feeling the weight lift off my shoulders. Like before, the voice came back, but it wasn't mine anymore. It was my sister's. That one line from a single conversation had been living rent-free in my head for years. We'd been having an argument, and on that day in particular I'd decided to stand up for myself instead of rolling over and hoping the conflict would end if I ignored it. After I'd advocated for myself, she said my reactions were explosive and unpredictable, that I had a certain wrath I would throw in anyone's direction when I was in that state. She wasn't compassionate in the description. She wasn't trying to understand why I might be having that kind of reaction, and it wasn't a moment when she was compassionately pointing that out to me so I could gain awareness of my apparent tendency to lash out. She was judging. I thought about that phrase. Was I violent, truly? Was I honestly a violent person? No, of course not. Did I have big reactions sometimes? Yes, I definitely did. Where did those reactions come from? I thought back to a time when she called me on it. If I were in a similar situation, in the grounded state I was in on the trail, would I have had the same response? Is that how I'd want to show up? No? Okay then, I dug for the root of that reaction. Was it mine? Was it something I internalized that I could unlearn?

I kept hiking and continued the exercise.

Okay, Sydney. Listen, you're definitely not violent. Are you kidding me? The girl that talks to flowers and hugs trees? Not violent. Also, the second you started standing up for yourself, all of a sudden she says you're violent? Sounds like she was uncomfortable with you having boundaries and wanted to keep you small. You didn't know what you didn't know. Now that you know that there is a difference between reactions and responses, and now that you know some of your triggers, you can handle these kinds of things better moving forward.

I stopped dead in my tracks and put my hands on my knees. It felt like another exorcism of sorts. Bent over, scream-crying at the ground, tears free-falling to the dusty trail between my feet. It felt like it had the other day—warm, bright, light, and floaty. Did I die . . . again?

I opened my eyes, and the sun had peeked through the clouds.

Okay, earth goddess warrior hiker chick, take it easy, I mocked myself.

Over the years I've internalized a lot of limiting and negative beliefs. Some of these come from the media I've consumed, some are conclusions I came to about myself, and some were said about me that really stuck. We kept hiking, and the process repeated over and over, with more of these one-liners. And every time, I repeated the process. It was a long slog of a hike. I had a lot of time to sort through it.

Here are some of the other negative bits that came up for me while we climbed toward Silver Peak:

> *You're too fat.*
> *You're too loud.*
> *You're too short to row varsity.*
> *Big girls like you will never be a flyer in a*
> * cheerleading stunt. You'll always be a base.*
> *Could you bring your first-date personality*
> * to this client meeting?*
> *If you want to make friends here, I suggest*
> * you tone down your enthusiasm.*
> *You're too young to do that.*
> *Every drop zone has a bicycle.*
> *This season, you're the bicycle.*

Everyone gets a ride.
You're such a slut.
If it's not your idea, you'll shut it down.
Nobody will ever love you.
You're such a bitch.
Are you sure you're stable enough to do this?
I could fuck him while you're gone.
You are disgusting.
I can't believe I slept with you.

I saw a path to a higher viewpoint and turned toward it, sprinting up the hill. By the time I got to the top I was out of breath, gasping for air. I had my hands on my head, trying to catch my breath and slow my heart down. I turned toward the ocean and stood there, looking out at the view while Barry made his way up to me. My whole body was vibrating. I asked Barry to take a picture of me. There wasn't a lot of room where we were, so I took up most of the frame. It wasn't the perspective I was looking for, but we didn't have many options. I posed, with my arms up, feeling electric. Not on fire, not uncomfortable, just hyperaware of my body and what it felt like to be alive. I was still trying to catch my breath. I could feel my lungs and my belly rise with the inhalations, and felt my whole body relax on the exhalations. My legs were twitching a little bit from the sprint up the hill. I felt sweat beading up under my lip, on the back of my neck, and between my breasts. My body was working. I could feel all of it. It was otherworldly.

The feeling was familiar, but different. There was another couple behind us and they joined us at the viewpoint. Perfect. I could actually get a picture of me and Barry.

We scooted back as far as we could, hoping maybe they'd have better luck with getting more of the scenery in frame. The sun was coming out, and I was so excited to have photos of that side of the island without an overcast sky.

While they tried to get different angles, I was holding a smile and thinking, *When was the last time I felt this good? When was the last time I felt this supported? When was the last time I felt this confident in my skin? When was the last time I felt this connected to my body? When was the last time I felt this capable?*

I popped a few electrolyte chews to keep my energy up on the descent into the Parsons Landing campground. The couple behind us hiked with us for a bit, and they said they were headed out to Starlight Beach. I wanted to hike out to Starlight, but if the downhill was anything like what the folks had described yesterday, I just wanted to get down to Parsons safely and enjoy the last campground for as long as we could.

We split at the fork for Starlight and turned toward Parsons Landing.

TRAIL OF LIFE

On that amazing day on the trail, I came face-to-face with my inner critic and told her and my limiting beliefs to take a hike. As my negative inner monologue played over and over and over again, enough was enough. I had been living with that soundtrack in my head for as long as I could remember. None of it was serving me. I thought back to something my skydiving coach had said when we first started working together: "Thoughts become things." If that were true, then I couldn't continue living that way.

Throwing my arms up to the sky and surrendering to whatever the trail has left to teach me.

Barry's grabbing my butt in this picture. Can you tell?

Then I remembered when I was in the dressing room before the first backpacking trip, standing in front of the mirror looking at a body I didn't recognize. "If you wouldn't dream of saying it to your best friend, don't say it to yourself."

While every topic under the sun is on the table for conversation with my friend, I don't ever speak to her the way I was speaking to myself in my head. I wanted to get to the bottom of it, so I remembered the course facilitator I mentioned before who'd said, "Let the negative thoughts go," like it's as easy as releasing a balloon from your hand and watching it float away. The limiting beliefs and negative thoughts we've been carrying for decades are going to require hard work and a boatload of compassion to work through and reframe, but it is possible.

If you grew up in a household or culture where showing your skin was equated with being slutty, easy, and *sinful,* it will be difficult to believe that you are allowed to wear whatever you want, however you want.

If you grew up in a home where family members constantly nagged you about your appearance, deciding to show up and show your face and your body exactly as you are—let alone being confident in doing so—can feel like the ultimate test of the foundational understanding you've been carrying.

If you were constantly told what to do, what you can't do, and didn't have anyone modeling what life on your own terms might look like, it can feel outright irresponsible and even life-threatening to give your dreams a shot.

All of which is to say we internalize a lot of messages from the people who raise us: our siblings and extended family, friends, media, and the culture at large. Deciding to show up in all of your glory exactly as you are in this moment will threaten the status quo. People don't know what to do with someone who doesn't need their approval. We're all so hardwired to be good and not rock the boat that when we find the confidence and courage to be 100 percent authentically *us,* it will challenge the very foundation of some of the people we're currently in community with.

Pardon my French, but fuck that noise.

Because as hard as it is for you to identify, reframe, and dig to the root of these beliefs that keep you playing small, it's going to be as difficult for the people in your life who *benefit* from you playing small to accept this.

Do. It. Anyway.

Your life literally depends on it. The life you've always wanted to live but are afraid to step into because you're unsure how the world will receive it is not going to show up without the work. You can walk to meet your future self, you can stand face-to-face, nose-to-nose with the life you know you deserve to live, but it is 100 percent up to you to take that next step.

I'm walking this walk with you. I see this happening for you.

The question is, can you see it for yourself?

Over the years since my first nudge to let my negative thoughts go, I learned more about visualization, intention-setting, and doing the deeply personal work of healing emotional trauma. I didn't have words for it yet, but across the island I had been releasing a lot of emotional pain and clearing space. When we release the stuff that has previously been taking up a lot of real estate in our brains (in my case, worrying about my thumbs, hair, and tattoos, for example), we have more energy to tackle whatever comes up next.

Let's unpack this process, shall we?

On the way toward Silver Peak, the highest point between Two Harbors and Parsons Landing, I realized just how much of the stuff in the trauma pack wasn't mine. It was the fears, insecurities, and projections of people I had interacted with over the course of my life. It's like they chucked all their heavy stuff in my bag without my knowledge or consent. I'm a kind woman, but I don't need to carry people's heavy stuff for them anymore. By the time I got to the top of that peak, I had tossed so much of the stuff that wasn't serving me out of my bag and replaced it with more love for myself, more compassion, more permission to continue to release these things as they come up for me.

Underneath all of the lies I had been feeding myself, I found the biggest, heaviest piece of trauma in my pack—the sexual assault. Once I cleared the way to get to my ooey-gooey center, my deepest, darkest secret, it wasn't so scary. Now I had so much practice speaking kindly to myself that by the time I got down to the sexual assault at the bottom of the trauma pack, hanging out in there like a cinder block, there was no way that discovery was going to take me down. Very quickly that piece of trauma became the brightest light and the biggest source of understanding, love, compassion, and empathy for myself and everything that happened in my life—good, bad, or indifferent— since the assault. It was only heavy when I didn't know what it was. I didn't see it until I was ready. And by the time I did, I knew what to do and how to handle it.

DEEPER DIVE

When you discover that you've been carrying things for other people, it might be tempting to call them out on it and pass their trauma back to them. That doesn't help anyone, and people don't like it when you give them their heavy stuff back. If they were capable of carrying it themselves or healing it altogether, they wouldn't have offloaded it on to you in the first place. Their healing is their responsibility, and it is entirely possible that they will never be able to heal. Some people genuinely don't know that they're doing this, but some people do. The folks that hurl insults your way intending to belittle you are doing so to have some measure of control—over you, over their own discomfort, or both. The fastest way to tell which side people are on is how they respond to your healing. As you grow and free yourself from the lies you've internalized as truth and allow your light to shine brightly, people will generally either be stoked for you or lash out in response to your liberation. Once those stories don't inform your every move, if the people in your life aren't rejoicing, they need healing. Folks who are committed to misery want you to be miserable, too, and they want you to pass it on like the common cold. It is your duty to yourself to break the cycle.

MINDFUL MILES

Let's dive deep and unpack those pesky negative thoughts together. Take a moment to acknowledge their presence, but remember, they don't define you. Give yourself permission to explore their origins and gently challenge their validity. Replace self-criticism with self-compassion as you peel back the layers. You are worthy of love and kindness, and these negative thoughts do not serve your highest good. Embrace the journey of releasing them, and step into a more empowered and positive mindset.

- What are the heavy items in your trauma pack that you've been carrying for other people?

- Do you have a negative internal soundtrack? What are some of the things you hear?

- When you hear these things, who is saying it? Is it your voice or someone else's?

- What would it feel like to release those beliefs? What if they didn't have power over you?

NEXT STEPS

Shortly after I left skydiving, I was enrolled in a women's entrepreneur-ship program and introduced to the term *inner mentor* as a balance to our inner critics. We did a visualization exercise led by Tara Mohr, author of *Playing Big,* during which she invited us to float high above our bodies into the ether and zoom forward through the space-time continuum until we meet ourselves twenty years down the road. I arrived at Future Sydney's house, where she invited me in, offered me a cucumber water, and showed me around. Her coastal home was taste-fully decorated with photos she'd taken on her adventures, artwork she'd created, and items she'd collected in her travels.

She took me to her writing room, complete with an ocean view and a perfectly cool breeze coming through the big bay windows. Her clothes were light, airy, and bohemian in nature, and she looked like the crunchiest granola goddess—flowing curly hair, slender and toned, a big smile, and bright eyes. I perused the shelf of her best-selling books, each one more successful than the last. She didn't say much to me in that visualization, but her presence was grounded, calming, and wise. Future Sydney really had her shit together, and I vowed to follow my heart and intuition with the hopes that I'd get to be her someday.

She was everything I wasn't at the time. She had an easy presence. Not carefree, because she clearly cared very deeply about a lot of things, but a quiet confidence. Like she genuinely knew everything would be okay. She was comforting in a way that felt like a blend of Mama Bear and best-friend energies mixed together. She was kind and she gave me a look like "You know what to do" before I left.

Whether you want to go for a hike with your future self, sit down with some journal prompts, or find a quiet spot to visualize, here are some prompts to help you get started:

- Imagine yourself traveling through time and space to meet yourself in twenty years.

- Where do you live? What is your home like?

- What does future you offer you when you arrive? Something to drink? A snack? A ten-course meal?

- What are you wearing? What do you look like?

- What are you doing with your life?

CHAPTER 16

IT'S ALL GOODE

Feeling the Flow

The couple who gave us the intel on the rest of the trail had been right. The descent into Parsons Landing was steep. My legs were exhausted from the climb to the top, my body was energized after feeling so alive once we got there, and my mind was seeking answers. I repeated the questions again in my mind.

When was the last time I felt this good? When was the last time I felt this supported? When was the last time I felt this confident in my skin? When was the last time I felt this connected to my body? When was the last time I felt this capable?

Barry was pretty far ahead of me, and I felt myself moving faster than I wanted to. I paused and dug in my poles. I closed my eyes and took a deep breath.

Hike your own hike.

I exhaled, opened my eyes, and started hiking again, taking smaller steps, using more caution, paying attention to where I was going. As long as I kept looking at my feet, I couldn't freak out about how steep that part of the trail was and how loose the ground was.

I thought about the times I felt comfortable in my body, before the trip.

2016, after we did the first hike.

2013, the first year I went to the USPA National Skydiving Championships.

2011, when I was running when we lived at the drop zone in Illinois.

"Comfortable in my body" was a bit of a stretch. At those points I didn't hate my body, but it was nothing close to how I felt then on the trail. I was at varying stages of indifference, with that first hike being the catalyst that launched my journey. That was different from the feeling I had on the trail. When was the last time I felt like this?

I kept my head down, as if the answer would be written in the loose gravel and dirt. Seeking. Looking for answers in the trail the same way I used to pray they'd be written at the bottom of a pint of Ben & Jerry's or a wine bottle.

When was the last time I felt this good?

I picked my head up to see where Barry was, and my foot started to slide out from under me. I dug in my poles, caught myself, and redistributed my weight. I took a deep breath and closed my eyes.

The last time I'd felt as good as I did then—as supported, as confident in my skin, as connected to my body, as capable—had been right before I was raped.

Standing, panting, braced as if I were traversing the gates of a downhill ski run, everything started to make sense. My pulse quickened. My mind was racing. If it were a cartoon, it would have sounded like a slot machine in my head. All of the chaotic parts of my life over the last twelve years were arranging themselves, and these fragmented parts of my life since the assault started to come into alignment. The assault was the missing puzzle piece.

If my brain were a computer, the only way I can describe what happened next was like downloading a massive folder of files on the fastest internet connection you can imagine and seeing little previews of the files as they're being downloaded. It felt like every movie sequence

I'd ever seen of someone's life flashing before their eyes. I thought maybe I had fallen down and hit my head, and it was a dream, but it wasn't. I was on the trail. Standing, leaning into my trekking poles, looking down at Parsons Landing, Barry far away in the distance. I was flooded with flashbacks from relationships, moments in classrooms, questionable decisions, arguments with people I loved, and reactions to things people have said to me over the years.

When I connected these dots, I wasn't scared and I wasn't sad. I felt free. For the first time in my life everything that felt out of character or chaotic or out of my control made sense. We still had quite a distance to go to get down to the campground. I shook my head, shook my hands out, and looked around. I wanted to take all of it in. I took some photos of where I was when I had my revelation, knowing it was one of the most important moments of my life. While I was looking through the camera's screen at the landscape ahead of me, I saw a hat hanging on a fence post.

I'm seconds away from posting a missed connection ad on Craigslist about the impact this hat had on me.

I tucked my camera back into my pack, got a grip on my poles, and sidestepped down the trail to get to the fence post. It was a cream-colored dad hat with white stitching proclaiming "It's All Goode." *What's with the "e"?* I got my phone out and took a picture of the hat. What the hell?

I looked around, wondering if I was actually Truman Burbank (Jim Carrey's character from *The Truman Show*) and this was my movie set. *Is someone messing with me?* I felt goose bumps head to toe and started crying. Not sad tears. Joy. Tears of pure joy. I was home. In my body. On the trail. With Barry. I had more confidence now. I didn't feel like I had to take itty-bitty baby steps. I took normal steps. It was steep, but it was starting to level out. As it did, I started skipping.

I thought about the bikini photo shoot I wanted to do with Barry in Little Harbor, which I ended up doing myself. I was disappointed that I hadn't asked him to take pictures that day, because the next day was overcast and didn't highlight Little Harbor in the same way. Overcast did not match how sunshiny I felt there. I had been through a lot since then. The thumbs? Hair? That whole big list of horrible things that I had internalized? No wonder I felt so amazing. I had just let go of a *lot* of stuff.

Bikini pictures didn't feel like enough. I wanted to run into the water fully naked. I wanted to give myself that gift. For the first time in a long time, I was at home in my body, and I knew why I wasn't before. I wanted documentation of me feeling that embodied. Plus, I thought about how when I'm old and gray, and things are hanging in different places, I want to remember how powerful my body has been, how powerful it *always* has been, at every stage of my life.

I shouted ahead to Barry. "Hey, when we get down there, I want to take off all my clothes and run into the ocean. I love my body, and I want pictures of me doing this. Will you be my cameraman?"

Barry stopped and turned around. The sun was behind me and shining in his eyes, so he lifted his arms to shield his face so he could see me.

"Hell yeah I'll be your cameraman!" he shouted back.

We made our way down the trail, connected with a road into the campground, and scoped the place out. We found our locker, grabbed the water and firewood we ordered, and walked over to our campsite.

"This beach just took over as my favorite place to camp on this island, if not in the world," I said.

We found our campsite, the last one on the left side of the lockers. We had the whole corner of the beach to ourselves. Hell, we had the whole *beach* to ourselves. There wasn't a soul in sight. We put our water in the fox box and left our packs out on the bench of the picnic table.

I unpacked my DSLR and handed it to Barry. I took off all of my clothes, took off my hat, and let my hair down, tucking my ponytail holder in my bag. I took off my rings, watch, and bracelet. The only thing that was on me that wasn't mine were my contact lenses. Since there was nobody else on the beach, I didn't grab my towel to take with me down to the water; I just marched my happy naked ass from the picnic table to the waves, free as a bird.

Barry followed me with the camera, clicking away.

I got to the ocean and paused. I looked around at the crystal-clear water, bright blue skies, and a bunch of seagulls pecking at the sand to my right. I started to walk into the waves, and by the time I was knee-deep I knew I was going to have to make it quick. The water was *coooold.* I had fallen off my board a few times last year, but other than that I hadn't spent much time in the ocean, so this was a surprise. I fully expected it to feel like the Caribbean. Nope. I waded out a bit further, up to mid-thigh. I let a few waves crash against my body, trying to reduce the shock as I walked out deeper. As the water went up to my belly button, a wave crashed and hit me right at the top of my shoulders.

Yep, far enough. I licked my lips, tasting the salty seawater as I did. I threw my arms up.

Hey, so I don't know what's up on this island, but this has been a pretty spiritual experience, I thought to myself, halfway talking to the universe, God, or whoever else might be listening. At that point I didn't know what the hell was going on, just that I was uncovering something big.

And if there's anything else for me to learn here, I'm open to it. I'm ready to receive it. As soon as I said, "receive it," I laughed to myself,

I was hoping for a *Little Mermaid* moment here, but I'll settle for the most impactful ocean dunk of my life.

remembering how disgusted I was by the end of that women's retreat when the speakers kept talking about manifesting your best life and abundance and being willing to receive.

Fuck me. I cannot believe I'm saying this shit. But if there's a shot in hell it works, then it's worth saying: Thank you, thank you, thank you, thank you. Whatever this was, I am so grateful for this experience, and I promise I'll do whatever it takes to keep learning and growing.

I lowered my arms, turned around, and looked back at Barry. He was still taking pictures. I turned back around, plugged my nose, and started to lower myself underwater. I dropped down to submerge my head, bumping my butt on the ocean floor. I hadn't walked out far enough. It was too cold. The abrupt stop to my dunking maneuver startled me, and I started a little limbo move as I ducked down to get my whole self under the water. I repositioned my feet to get stable, popping back up to stand in waist-high water. I rubbed the saltwater out of my eyes and smoothed my hair back.

When I opened my eyes everything seemed a bit sharper. The colors were more vibrant. Like someone had dehazed my field of vision.

As I looked out to the ocean in front of me, I knew that I had been hiking my feelings. That much was abundantly clear. But in that moment, in that water, and at those pivotal points along the second hike, I was reclaiming my body. Reclaiming it from the people who said it wasn't good enough, or that it needed to be fixed to fit in a very narrow standard of beauty. Reclaiming it from the man who had assaulted me.

In that moment, I was rebirthed.

TRAIL OF LIFE

When I share this part of the story, I get full body goose bumps, because this was one of those moments where life just clicks. We have so many opportunities to be hard on ourselves, to wish things were different, that we often breeze right by these moments. It is my hope that by making it this far into this book that you feel well equipped to connect the dots on your own life.

To get to electric alignment, that feeling of flow, where everything feels like it's happening so naturally, we must be honest with ourselves. We must face the scariest monsters under our beds and in our closets. We are expert avoiders of feeling feelings, so this requires not only a lot of self-awareness, but also compassion and permission to release judgment about whatever got in our way to begin with. Once again it is important to remember that the awareness is the work. You cannot skip over becoming aware, having these hard conversations with yourself, or spending time understanding the physical sensations and emotions you will feel. If you've been numbing with alcohol or drugs or obsessive workouts or constant distractions, just feeling the feelings instead of avoiding them is the work. If it feels like you got hit by a freight train, congratulations, you're doing the work. Just keep making notes in the margins of this book, keep journaling, keep listening to your body, and pay attention to how good it feels when you lighten your load.

Hiking was the thing that helped me take these practices that felt so out of touch and apply them to my life. I was never explicitly taught that once we choose to let thoughts go that they'll never return. But because there wasn't any nuance or depth to this lesson when I learned it—it was simply a tactic that one particular facilitator used to release their negative thoughts—I assumed this practice was a one-and-done kind of thing. So of course I would get frustrated whenever those thoughts came back.

When I'm in alignment—balanced, feeling healthy in my body, clear-headed, and grounded—I know the following to be true:

- My light is bright.

- I'm damn good at my work.

- My body is a powerhouse.

What is possible when I know these things in my bones? What pulls me away from that knowing?

I liken the thoughts that float through my head to being on a river. When I'm meditating, on-trail, writing, or otherwise creatively or phys-ically present and engaged, the river is slow and serene. The thoughts come floating by on their inflatables, and I observe them as they pass. This is when some of my best ideas present themselves, and from this place I adopt them with confidence.

When I'm out of alignment it feels like we're approaching the rapids. It's chaotic, loud, and I just lost my paddle. There are frat bros on dick-shaped inflatables shouting absurdities at full volume, and they're playing awful music. If I don't flee the scene, I try to regain some sense of control. I dive into the water, tackle a raft, and try to steer it away from the rapids. More often than not, when a negative thought would come around the river bend, I'd latch on to it and try to prove to myself that the thought wasn't true. Now I see these wild thoughts as clues. They aren't something to be tamed, disproven, or wrangled—just data. A hint that something is amiss in my normally serene and peaceful center.

To unpack my lazy river and turn this into a practice you can use, I start with the awareness of a thought: Where does this come from? My voice? Someone else's?

Does it sound like "I'm so bad" or "You're so bad"? If it sounds like you're saying this to yourself and you've committed to being your own best friend (and therefore wouldn't say something like this to yourself), sometimes that awareness can be enough to release the thought. If it's someone else's voice, that can help you tap into the memory that brought this up. Sometimes it's both. When I was on the mountain, sometimes it sounded like my voice first, and after I released it, it would come back and sound like the person who'd actually said it.

After you've identified the thought, what would it feel like to release it? How much time have you spent hearing this and doing nothing about it? You have the rest of your beautiful life to unlearn these things and replace them with the thoughts that fill your soul. Throughout this book I've provided prompts and practices to help you release in various ways. Now let's talk about why I love hiking for the actual practice of releasing.

I do a lot of thinking about releasing thoughts and when it's time to put in the work to release. This is a practice I do exclusively when I'm in motion, because my body holds stories of unworthiness, and when I start to challenge my body, or when I'm in my body that can do these things, those stories come out with a vengeance. This is why I hike. Before I started hiking, I would try to process my pain, and I'd get stuck when my body would react with fight-or-flight symptoms. I didn't have anywhere to put that energy, so I would just shut down and stop doing the work to heal. Sometimes, it would take days, weeks, months, or even years to return to whatever I was trying to process. Once I started hiking, everything changed. Now, I have somewhere to put that burst of energy.

The harder the hike, the more likely it is that I'll have something to process. And as it turns out, I can hike through the emotional discomfort. That fight-or-flight response that comes from remembering these things gives me a burst of energy when I'm climbing a mountain. I can expel that negative energy from my body into the mountain, and leave the weight of the negativity behind.

When you hear similar thoughts, where do they come from? Would your highest self speak to you in this way? Would you talk to your BFF that way? If a thought is so preposterous and now you can see it, don't even give it the time of day for understanding and reframing. Let that shit go. However, if it's something that has lived rent-free in your head, know that it's 100 percent okay if it takes more than one hike to do this.

The idea is to feel through the releasing of the thought, and pay attention to how good it feels when you allow it to pass through you versus getting stuck in your body. When you feel incredible, hold on to that. Savor it. Cherish it. Make note of what it feels like. As you get more in tune with the joy and the elation, you can more easily recognize it when it shows up in your life in other ways from other sources. That physical sensation is a permission slip to remember all the work you've done and how good it feels to do it.

Do this enough and you'll soon be looking forward to releasing the emotional weight. Voila! Your mental health is improving and so is your physical health because of the frequency and the mindset you're coming to the activity with. Doesn't it feel better to say, "I hike to heal" versus "Let's go to the mountain and punish ourselves because hiking is hard and I hate my body"? The special sauce happens when you know how freeing it is to live without the voice, even if that feeling is temporary at first.

Are you willing to feel this good all the time? Are you okay with feeling this way more than not? Because if you aren't ready to receive the blessings of this practice, you'll miss them. Be ready to receive what you hope for.

MINDFUL MILES

Ready to unlock the magic and feel the flow? To tap into that incredible state, you gotta find your sweet spot. What lights you up? What makes time disappear? What makes you feel at home in your body? That's your key. Take it to the trail and use the prompts below to focus on the people, places, and activities that ignite your passion. Get lost in the rhythm, embrace the challenge, and let go of your distractions. When you fully immerse yourself, you'll find yourself in that glorious state of flow where your potential knows no bounds. Get ready to ride the wave of inspiration!

- Think back to the last time you felt on fire, like everything was aligned. What happened after that?

- When was the last time you stood in awe of your body and what it can do?

- Do you believe in something bigger than yourself? What is it? What does it stand for?

NEXT STEPS

Healing is a lifelong journey, and we have the rest of our lives to do this work. We cannot do everything all at once, nor should we try to. It's not possible, it's not necessary, and it will only cause us more pain and frustration. So I invite you to settle into your healing journey and get comfortable. This is going to be a long, beautiful, and wild ride.

While I'd argue that doing this work ultimately leads to joy, I know firsthand how difficult it is when you're in the thick of it. To balance out the deep emotional processing, it's important to focus on joy and rest.

First let's focus on joy. Think back to when you were a kid, before you had all the responsibilities you do now. What made you happy? What brought you joy? Was it playing outside? Coloring in a coloring book? Making music or art? Make a list of the things that have brought you joy throughout your life, and each week do at least one of those things. Set a date. Give yourself something to look forward to.

When it comes to rest, don't wait until your body starts to shut down to take the rest you need. There are a lot of life factors that are thirsty for our time and attention, and you can't pour from an empty cup.

At some point every day, I invite you to sit with yourself and ask yourself what you need. Listen to what comes up and take action. If the action is resting, please listen to your body and allow it to rest. You are a gift to this world, and we cannot experience the full beauty of your presence if you're not resting and taking care of yourself. If you need it, consider this your official permission to set down the backpack, set down the processing, turn your phone off, and take a damn nap.

You deserve it.

COMING HOME

The sunset after my rebirth ceremony was incredible. That night we sat by the campfire and watched for shooting stars, cowboy camping on the beach. The waves lapping on the rocks were the perfect white noise to ease me into one of the best nights of sleep I had gotten in over a decade, since the assault. I was safe, happy, free, loved.

The next morning we woke up and it was overcast again. As we packed up camp, I didn't want to leave.

Can we stay here? I thought. *I could live here. I've got everything I need, and I could just go back and forth to Two Harbors every few days to stock up on snacks and supplies.*

It really did feel like a victory lap, and as we passed mile marker thirty-three of the Trans-Catalina Trail, I paused and cried. That was the mile marker I had been most looking forward to on the trail—celebrating the farthest I had ever hiked, my thirty-third birthday, and a new commitment to myself from the trip moving forward. I did it. I knew I could do it. And if I could do that, what else was possible?

For the last five miles, I skipped and cried as we made our way back into the town of Two Harbors. I wanted to sprint because I was so excited, and I wanted to stop and sit down because I didn't want the experience to end. Barry and I stopped right before the last turn into town and hugged.

"Proud of you," he said one last time, hands on my face. He pulled me in for a kiss.

I sniffled so my boogers wouldn't interfere with the kiss. "I'm proud of me too," I whimpered through my tears.

While I knew I had learned a lot about myself on this trip, I also knew there was a lot of work ahead of me. This was a big step in my healing journey, and I knew it wasn't the last.

In the years that have passed since that second trek across Catalina Island, Barry and I sold everything we owned and moved into a van old enough to buy beer, a 1998 Chevy named Ruby. We have been traveling around the United States, hosting hundreds of events about our experience on the TCT—including talks at sixty REI stores—and we introduced thousands of people to the healing power of nature through our non-profit, Hiking My Feelings (you can learn more about our programs and events in the "Join the Community" section at the end of the book). I am so grateful that I said yes to Barry's invitation to experience the great outdoors, took a chance on myself, took responsibility for my healing, and kept showing up, even when— *especially* when—it was hard.

As Adam would say, you only get so many sunsets. This one at Parsons Landing didn't disappoint.

Looking back, I wouldn't change anything that happened to me—not even that morning of the rape—because I can see now that every twist and turn on my Trail of Life has brought me to this place, right here, right now. It is easy to fall into a victim mindset and wear your pain like a weighted blanket. For decades I had been stuck in survival mode, completely oblivious to how a single moment in time had influenced every decision I was making. It wasn't until I went hiking and started unpacking my trauma pack that I started to feel empowered by the process instead of waiting until I had tangible results.

While this story ends on a high note, the work isn't done. I thought the sexual assault was the last thing in my trauma pack, and while I knew I still had a lot of healing and unpacking to do, I genuinely thought that was the last thing I needed to heal. On the trail and in life we experience peaks and valleys, but that doesn't mean that climbing uphill will be tough forever or that going downhill in our low times is a bad thing. These are both parts of the journey; neither is inherently positive or negative, and if you tap into the resources shared within these pages, I am confident that you too can transform your pain into power.

As much as I wish that the TCT fixed me and that life would be sunshine and rainbows for the rest of my days, that isn't the case. Trauma still sneaks up on me, but now I have the tools to self-soothe and remind myself that while my body might be remembering the trauma, I am in fact safe. From time to time, I think about how many lives I could have saved as a surgeon if I hadn't been derailed from going to medical school. Perhaps I would have found a cure for cancer. Maybe I would have invented some revolutionary procedure or technique that could have changed the way we approach medicine. When those thoughts come up, I honor them as potent reminders of how far I've come. I know I'm lucky that my pivot in my studies took me where it did, and that I'm able to share this story with you now. I'm lucky that what fell apart in the aftermath of the worst day of my life was largely academic, and that it wasn't a gateway to more trauma.

Because trauma is a gateway drug.

Read that again.

Many people who experience trauma turn to drugs or alcohol to cope with their distressing emotions and memories, me included. Drinking gave me temporary relief from the painful thoughts and feelings associated with the assault, and later the grief of losing twenty-three friends in four years, the stress of my career, and more. However, the use of drugs or alcohol can quickly turn into a pattern of addiction, as the brain's reward system becomes rewired to seek out the pleasurable effects of the substance. If it weren't for my diabetes diagnosis, I wouldn't have had the opportunity to see my story from a new perspective. You don't have to hit rock bottom to make different choices. You can choose healing whenever you're ready.

When it comes to conversations about trauma, we can no longer be silent. I'm not saying you must sell everything you own, move into a van, sacrifice every creature comfort while you learn how to share your story, and then shout it from the mountaintops. But at the very least, we must break the silence with ourselves and with the people who care about us.

This book, my work, and living my life out loud is how I'm breaking my silence. I know that when I share my story I am providing language that may help others articulate what happened to them. Every time I hesitate to share, every time I'm on the brink of silencing myself, I stop and think about how everything and everyone good in my life is the result of me taking responsibility for my healing. I strive every day to be the human Little Sydney needed but hadn't met yet.

I grew up in a tight-knit Midwestern household. We told each other everything, but I didn't feel safe telling them about the assault when it happened, so I swore myself to silence. After I got done with the second hike and had context for everything I had been through, I shared the discoveries I had made on-trail with my family. While I wish this part of the story ended in a big family hug, a ton of understanding, and endless support, it doesn't. Sharing my story uncovered another piece of trauma in my invisible backpack—generational trauma.

As soon as I shared my revelations with them, I felt a negative shift in our family dynamic. My father seemed to change within seconds. After I finished sharing my story with him for the first time in its entirety, he cut me off, going on to say that my story about being raped was bullshit and I better come up with a new one, because nobody was buying the story I was telling. His reaction was confirmation of my choice to keep this story to myself, because if I had come home that day after the assault, told him, and received that reaction, I can guarantee I wouldn't be alive or writing this book today. I wouldn't have survived that.

I share this because sometimes the people you trust to have your back won't be able to show up for you because they are incapable of showing up for themselves. For as much as my father had an explosive temper at times, I also grew up thinking he was my best friend. I'm fortunate that by the time I had shared this with him, I knew that his reaction was about him, not about me. Still, I got curious about his reaction and started to put the pieces together. Through some stories my mother shared about our family history and a handful of aha moments from conversations with friends who had experienced similar family dynamics in the face of shocking news, it became abundantly clear to me—this was generational trauma.

Some of the trauma we carry is generational, and it gets passed down again and again through our silence. Our bodies retain it, store it, and know it. And it's not until someone decides to disrupt the pattern and break the silence—even if only with themselves—that the cycle stops.

If trauma can be passed down generation to generation, so can healing.

I am child free by choice. This book and our organization are the closest thing I'll ever have to children of my own, so I choose to keep speaking up. I won't be silenced. What happened to me isn't my fault, and what happened to you isn't your fault. I'm done living a life in the shadows of my pain. I didn't come this far to *only* come this far; I have a lot of life I want to live, and if it doesn't make sense to anyone else, that's fine. I'm here to hike my own hike and share stories along the way. It is my hope that doing so breaks the cycle for me in this life, and I hold the vision of the day that my family comes to see how doing so has led me to the happiest and healthiest life I've ever known. Because if all of this is true for me, it's true for you as well.

If you're reading this and you've survived some hard things, hi. Welcome to the next chapter of your life. If you've found some of your story within these pages, know that it's because we're all way more alike than we are different. I'm sorry if my words have caused you pain, but the fact that you're able to feel is one of the most beautiful parts of the human experience. There is no shame in crying, screaming, and curling up in the fetal position. I won't take it personally if my story stirs up feelings in you that are terrifying and make you want to burn this book.

I will say this: I see you. I hear you. I believe you. I love you. You can do this. Together *we* can do this. And know this much—I've got your back.

If there's any chance you're like me, I need you to hear this loud and clear. If you've been reading this, nodding a lot, and you feel like my story is your story, that's because it is. We are all one. We are all part of a collective consciousness. Unity is power, and our lived experiences are ours and are unique to us, but the major through lines of our stories are shared. Whether you believe in the universe, God, unicorns, the flying spaghetti monster, or anything in between, at the end of the day we are all mirrors for each other. If you're inspired and want to find this kind of healing, to know yourself this well, all you have to do now is recognize that you are worthy of embodying these qualities. You see these qualities in the people you look up to because you already hold them within yourself.

At the end of the day we're all just walking each other home. If you take some time with the resources available in this book, I know that you will find a way home to yourself time and time again. If it's possible for me to take the worst day of my life and turn it into something that makes the world a better place, what else is possible? For me, for you, for all of us?

SUPPORT RESOURCES

If you or someone you know is a survivor of sexual assault, is having suicidal thoughts, or is concerned about their risk factors for diabetes and are in need of support, the following organizations are a great place to start:

Rape, Abuse & Incest National Network (RAINN)
Call 800-656-4673
Visit www.rainn.org

988 Suicide & Crisis Lifeline
Call 988
Visit www.suicidepreventionlifeline.org

American Diabetes Association
Visit www.diabetes.org

JOIN THE COMMUNITY

You've read the book. Now it's time to do the work. If I'm going to spend all these pages writing about how hiking helped me heal my mind and body, I don't just want you to take my word for it. I want you to experience this healing firsthand for yourself.

After our first tour around the United States in 2018 and 2019, I didn't feel alone on an island anymore. We met people from all over the world who were feeling big feelings and finding healing on the trail. When we got home from that first tour, we took what had started as an Instagram handle and a hashtag and turned Hiking My Feelings into a nonprofit organization. Every day, we put one foot in front of the other toward our mission: to improve community health by creating opportunities for people to experience the healing power of nature.

While my story serves as the foundation for all of the programs and experiences I've developed over the years, this is bigger than me. Our programs and wilderness experiences combine physical activity with emotional healing. We encourage people to explore their feelings and work through emotional pain while enjoying the beauty of nature. To take it one step further, whenever possible, we build our programming around a conservation project. By tailoring our activities and work-shops to the needs of the spaces we are occupying, we are able to connect the dots between our inner and outer wilderness and we bring healing to the lands that help us heal.

When you're ready, we'd love to welcome you into our community of big-hearted adventurers and walk with you on your Trail of Life. Here's how to stay connected with us:

Hiking My Feelings

Visit hikingmyfeelings.org

Blaze Your Own Trail to Self-Love

Visit hikingmyfeelings.org/byot

This workshop series is where we lace up our hiking boots and venture deep into the wilderness of self-discovery, embracing an empowering mindset and the practices that will set your heart ablaze. Join us as we navigate the rugged terrain of limiting beliefs, scale the mountains of self-compassion, and uncover the hidden treasures of self-acceptance. Together, we will forge a new path, igniting a fierce love for ourselves that will radiate through every aspect of our lives.

Wilderness Wellness Retreats

Visit hikingmyfeelings.org/retreats

Escape to a world where breathtaking landscapes and soul-stirring adventures meet profound self-discovery. Welcome to our Wilderness Wellness retreats, where nature becomes your healing sanctuary and transformation unfolds with each step. Join us on an immersive journey as we explore majestic trails, embrace mindfulness practices, and unlock the power of our emotions. Dive deep into the wilderness of your heart, nourish your spirit, and forge lifelong connections. Are you ready to embark on an unforgettable retreat that will ignite your senses and leave you forever changed? By reading this book, you already have a foundational understanding of how we do what we do. Let's put it into practice together!

Wellness in the Wilderness Podcast

Visit hikingmyfeelings.org/wellness

Welcome to the *Wellness in the Wilderness* podcast, where we venture deep into the untamed beauty of nature to uncover the secrets of holistic well-being. Join me as we engage in captivating conversations with experts from all walks of life, discovering how the wilderness can be a transformative catalyst for personal growth and inner balance. Get ready to immerse yourself in inspiring stories, practical tips, and the soothing serenity of the great outdoors. Tune in and let nature guide you on a path to vibrant wellness and profound connection.

Additional Resources

Visit hikingmyfeelings.org/book to find supplementary resources for this book, including a list of our favorite communities who are making the outdoors more inclusive.

ACKNOWLEDGMENTS

Millions of years ago, two tectonic plates smushed together to form an island approximately twenty-two miles long off the coast of Los Angeles, California. The Tongva were the first people there, and they named the island Pimu. For at least eight thousand years, they stewarded its rolling hills, vast canyons, and ocean waters. While there is no way for us to ever hear the stories of healing and thriving on this land directly from its first people, I can feel the energy of those who walked this path before me with every step and every breath I take on this land. I've heard that the island always gives you what you need, and that has been true for me in all of the time I've spent there, either as a visiting hiker or as a resident.

My connection to the landmass currently known as Santa Catalina Island started with the Trans-Catalina Trail, so I am deeply grateful to Kevin Ryan for building the trail, Laura Minuto for mapping the trail, and the employees, board members, and volunteers at the Catalina Island Conservancy who took the seed of an idea for a trail that spanned the island and turned it into one of the most unique backpacking destinations in the world.

To the Hiking My Feelings board members and program facilitators, Aaron Strout, Gabaccia Moreno, Mary Ramenofsky, Michelle Zilinskas, Laurie Sweets, and euni: Thank you for bringing your magic to our organization and for your guidance and friendship. It is a privilege to be in your orbit.

To our sponsors and partners, Becky Marcelliano, John Holdmeier, Ethan O'Keefe, Grant Sible, Sarah del Puerto, Max Pringle, Andrew Glenn, Travis Avery, and Kim Safdy: Thank you for believing in what we're building at Hiking My Feelings. Your support has been instrumental to the health of our organization and empowers us to make a difference every day.

To Sue and Dustan at the Reggae Ranch: Simply put, this ship woulda sunk in 2020 if it weren't for your generosity. We are forever grateful for the opportunity to call the Reggae Ranch home and make some incredible memories there with you and the family. Thank you for always being a soft place to land and a firm place to launch from between tours and events. We love you!

To Melanie and Kaleo Wassman: Thank you for being you and for being so open with your hearts and energy. It is an honor to cocreate with you. Thank you for saying yes to our wild ideas. Thank you for loving us.

To Craig McKnight: Thank you for being my first call on so many milestones and meltdowns over the years. Your capacity to lead, build community, and keep putting one foot in front of the other for Muffin But Good Vibes inspires me when it feels impossible to continue.

Music is a big part of what we do at Hiking My Feelings and we are grateful for the love, support, and encouragement from Kaleo Wassman, Tomboyce Avenue, Nicholas Dell, Brendan Dane, Derek Waldmann, Chris Bowen, Scott Woodruff, Kevin Bong, Johnny Cosmic, Karim Israel, Aaron Wolf, Dubbest, Brendan Clemente, Nathan Feinstein, Joshua Swain, Matthew Goodwin, Stephen "Zumbi" Gaines, Nattali Rize, Howi Spangler, Brett Wilson, Kyle Smith,

Spencer and Evan Burton, The Late Ones, and Kaleidoscope Kid. Between our events online, on the road, and on the trail, we are so thankful for your music, as it has brought great healing to our community and to me personally as well. Thank you for being the soundtrack to our movement.

To Kevin Wong, Misha Askren, Ann Murdy, Robin Balch, Sarah Witt, Benny Lopez, Jon Norris, and the rest of the volunteers and team at the Joshua Tree National Park Association: Thank you for seeing the vision, giving me the opportunity to develop programming for the Desert Institute, and supporting our events in the park.

To Katie Wightman, Tim Barrett, Jonathan Humphrey, Tori Ramirez, Daniel Huecker, and the rest of the volunteers and team at Sequoia Parks Conservancy, Sequoia National Park, and the Volunteers-In-Parks program: It is an honor to continue the history of healing in Sequoia National Park with you. Thank you for the opportunity to bring healing to the lands that help us heal.

This beautiful book would not have come to life in this way without a side-stage conversation with Jayashri Triolo—gushing about retreats and nature and wellness—which led to an introduction to Susan McCarthy at Mandala Springs Wellness Retreat Center. My life changed the moment I stepped out of the van and onto the property. If it weren't for that big red banner above the office door, I wouldn't have met Phillip Jones, and eventually Raoul Goff, from Insight Editions/MandalaEarth. Thank you all for sharing the stoke for this story.

To the *Hiking Your Feelings* book team, starting with Katie Killebrew and Amanda Nelson: Thank you for the opportunity to share this story far and wide! To my soulful editors, Tania Casselle and Peter Adrian Behravesh: Thank you for holding my hand, cheering me on, and slicing and dicing this thing into the work of art it is today. My gratitude also extends to the other incredible humans at MandalaEarth and Insight Editions who have ushered this book into the world with me. Thank you.

Gratitude speed round: Kat Humphus, Melanie and Aaron Strout, Lydia and Howard Williams, Linda Rubin, Laura Bingaman, Christine Shirinian, Brandi Blazier, and Michelle LeRoy. I love you. Thank you for hyping me up, catching me when I fall, offering your wisdom, and loving me, even when—*especially* when—I'm difficult to love.

Ultimately, none of this would be possible without the love, snuggles, and support from my devastatingly handsome husband and best friend, Barry Williams. You are my partner in everything we do, my adventure buddy for life, and my coach, always. Thank you for having my back, for catching all the cobwebs on our early morning hikes, and for suggesting we go backpacking back in 2016. This is the best chapter of my life, and there is nobody else I'd rather share these experiences with than you.

Last, but most definitely not least, I wanna thank me.

I've had a lot of support, as this acknowledgments section indicates. But at the end of the day, my healing is my responsibility. I can have all the privilege and all the resources and all the information to make solid choices, but when it comes down to it, it's me, myself, and I doing this work. So, to Little Sydney, who has always felt a bit out of place, a little "too much" for most, and has always known, deep down, that we are destined for greatness: I got your back. Never stop telling me when something hurts. I might not always know what to do, and you might have to tell me a few times to get me to pay attention, but I promise I will always do the best I can to ensure that you know you are safe, you are protected, and you are free to shine as brightly as you want.

ABOUT THE AUTHOR

Sydney Williams is the founder of Hiking My Feelings®, a nonprofit organization dedicated to the healing power of nature. Her fifteen-year (and counting) career in communications has run the gamut from launching Oscar Mayer's social media channels and working with Fortune 500 brands to educating the public about the importance of stewardship and equitable access to recreational opportunities. Through it all, she centers empathetic storytelling and allows her curiosity and enthusiasm to lead the way.

Sydney has been featured in *HuffPost*, *Psychology Today*, *U.S. News & World Report*, and on the SXSW stage. She is also a certified Wilderness First Responder, an instructor at the Desert Institute at Joshua Tree National Park, an instructor at the Field Institute at Sequoia National Park, and a founding member of the Outdoorist Oath. Sydney has been nominated for Woman of the Year by *San Diego Magazine.*

MANDALA

An imprint of MandalaEarth
PO Box 3088
San Rafael, CA 94912
www.MandalaEarth.com

Find us on Facebook: www.facebook.com/MandalaEarth
Follow us on Twitter: @MandalaEarth

Publisher Raoul Goff
Associate Publisher Phillip Jones
Publishing Director Katie Killebrew
Editor Peter Adrian Behravesh
Editorial Assistant Amanda Nelson
VP, Creative Director Chrissy Kwasnik
Art Director Ashley Quackenbush
Senior Designer Stephanie Odeh
VP Manufacturing Alix Nicholaeff
Production Manager Joshua Smith
Sr Production Manager, Subsidiary Rights Lina s Palma-Temena

MandalaEarth would also like to thank Tania Casselle, Bob Cooper, and Jessica Easto for their work
on this book.

ISBN: 979-8-88762-084-8

Manufactured in China by Insight Editions
10 9 8 7 6 5 4 3 2 1

Insight Editions, in association with Roots of Peace, will plant two trees for each tree used in the manufacturing
of this book. Roots of Peace is an internationally renowned humanitarian organization dedicated to eradicating
land mines worldwide and converting war-torn lands into productive farms and wildlife habitats. Roots of Peace
will plant two million fruit and nut trees in Afghanistan and provide farmers there with the skills and support
necessary for sustainable land use.